MUSLIMS IN INDIA

MUSLIMS IN INDIA

Edited by
S.N. SINGH

ANMOL PUBLICATIONS PVT. LTD.
NEW DELHI - 110 002 (INDIA)

ANMOL PUBLICATIONS PVT. LTD.
4374/4B, Ansari Road, Daryaganj
New Delhi - 110 002
Ph.: 23261597, 23278000
Visit us at: www.anmolpublications.com

Muslims in India

First Published, 2003

ISBN 81-261-1427-4

PRINTED IN INDIA

Published by J.L. Kumar for Anmol Publications Pvt. Ltd., New Delhi - 110 002 and Printed at Mehra Offset Press, Delhi.

CONTENTS

PART – III: GENERAL

PART—III: GENERAL

PREFACE

There is no denying the fact that Muslims constitute the majority amongst the minorities and are the second largest community in India. In view of their sheer number their role in the overall socio-economic development can hardly be over-emphasised. However, the last five decades of planned development do not show very encouraging picture so far as the Muslim community in India is concerned. Their participation in the political process has been taken advantage of by several political formations, with little benefits in real terms going to the community. This is not to argue that other communities got benefited at the cost of Muslim communities or that the rest of India progressed, but Muslims did not. Lack of development for different sections of the Indian society may call for different explanations, as are the reasons for regional imbalances. Taking into account the problems faced by the Muslims in India and the nature of state intervention thereof, a national seminar was organised by the Institute for Applied Research and Development, Lucknow sometime back. The seminar generated considerable debate during the sessions as well as in the media. In order to give this debate a wider circulation and coverage, the papers contributed in the seminar are being published in a book form. It is hoped that the book will reach the wider sections and generate further debate for the betterment of the community and the country at large. Also it should be able to address the present concerns in the Indian polity. Many of us feel that the country at present is passing through critical phases and issues such as this can be ignored only at its own peril. In view of the seriousness of the issue it is hoped that it should be able to attract the thinking minds which would go a long way to help the general cause.

ACKNOWLEDGEMENTS

Several people have helped in the successful conduct of the national seminar. It is my bounden duty to express my thanks and gratefulness to such people who provided me help and support during the course of the seminar without which it would not have been possible for me to organise such an event. While it may not be possible to mention here the names of each and every person, though one would very much like to, certain organisations and individual do need a special mention. First of all I would like to thank the Indian Council of Social Science Research, New Delhi, for the financial assistance provided to organise the national seminar. I am thankful to Hon'ble Justice (Rtd.) Sri H.N. Tilhari, Chairman Backward Class Commission, U.P. for his kindly inaugurating the seminar and Sri T.N. Dhar, I.A.S. (Rtd.) for kindly presiding over the inaugural session. I express my thanks to Hon'ble Justice (Rtd.) Sri H.A. Raza, presently Lok Ayukta, Uttaranchal, for kindly giving the valedictory Address and Professor S.B. Singh, Vice-Chancellor, University of Lucknow, for kindly presiding over the function. I am thankful to Professor C.P. Barthwal, Head, Department of Public Administration, Lucknow University for his help in the conduct of the seminar as well as for participation in the deliberation of the seminar. I express my thanks to all the participants, whose papers enriched the deliberations in the seminar. My thanks are due to the office bearers of the Institute particularly Sri S. Saran, Dr. Kamal Srivastava, and Dr. S.S. Chauhan whose persistent efforts made the seminar a success. I am thankful to all the contributors for their generous support. My thanks are due to media persons for efficient coverage of the seminar. In the end my thanks to Mr. Pramod Kumar for nice computer typing the manuscript and to Anmol Publications Pvt. Ltd., New Delhi for publishing this volume in record time.

—*SNS*

LIST OF CONTRIBUTORS

1. Professor S.N. Singh, Professor, Department of Public Administration, Lucknow University and Secretary of IARD.
2. Mohd. Haleem Khan, IAS, Secretary, Government of U.P., Lucknow.
3. Professor Saleem Akhtar, Ex. Dean and Chairman, Department of Law, Aligarh Muslim University, Aligarh.
4. Mr. Nafees Ahmed, LLM, Lecturer, Department of Law, Aligarh Muslim University, Aligarh.
5. Dr. Kumkum Kishore, Reader, Department of Public Administration, Lucknow University.
6. Dr. S.S.A. Jafri, Senior Fellow, Giri Institute of Development Studies, Lucknow.
7. Professor M. Muzzammil, Professor, Department of Economics, Lucknow University.
8. Dr. Shashi Shukla, Reader, Department of Political Science, Lucknow University.
9. Dr. Ramesh Madan, Assistant Director, Indian Council of Social Science Research, New Delhi.
10. Dr. Vaishali Saxena, Lecturer (Part-Time) Department of Public Administration, Lucknow University.
11. Dr. S.P. Misra, Senior Faculty and Consultant, Institute of Development Studies, Lucknow University.
12. Sri Abhinav Sharma, Senior Research Fellow, Department of Public Administration, Lucknow University.

13. Dr. Noor Mohammad, IAS, Secretary and Chief Electoral Officer of U.P.
14. Ms. Abhilasha Srivastava, Senior Research Fellow, Department of Sociology, Lucknow University.
15. Dr. Awadhesh Kumar Singh, Senior Faculty, Institute of Development Studies, Lucknow University.
16. Dr. S.R. Rastogi, Former Additional Director/Professor, Population Research Centre, Lucknow University, Lucknow.
17. Ms. Seema Parveen, Associated with Solidarity of The Nation Society (NGO), Gonda, Uttar Pradesh.
18. Professor Jag Mohan Singh Verma, Professor and Head, Department of Sociology, Lucknow University.
19. Dr. K.K. Srivastava, Research Faculty, Department of Public Administration, Lucknow University.
20. Professor S.K. Singh, Professor, Department of Public Administration, Lucknow University.
21. Sri Amitabh Thakur, IPS, Special Enquiry, Jawahar Bhawan, Lucknow.

INTRODUCTION

The modern India marked a departure from its earlier history so far as the socio-political paradigms were concerned. The Preamble of the Constitution stands a testimony to this philosophy of governance. The socialist secular Republic envisaged a different life for all its citizens irrespective of class, caste, sex, religion etc. however, how far these national goals and objective have been fulfilled and achieved remains at best a matter of long debate. In this context, the question of the Muslim minorities who constitute a significant percentage of India's population after Hindus too remain a question of debates. It has also been argued that India's long standing efforts to uplift its disadvantaged or backward sections through group based policies offers many lessons from which the rest of the world might learn.[1] India's Muslim are also addressed as large of a divided nation.[2] The administration in India too is seen as having a legacy of the British. In spite of these, one can argue that there was complete commitment on the part of nation builders of modern India towards the goal of growth and development for all. Emanating from these efforts, there has been growth in different sectors. However, doubts are expressed about the equitable distribution of the fruits of the development. The seminar debated some of the issues concerned with Muslim minorities in this context.

There is no controversy about the fact that Muslim of India in general are a backward community whatever criteria one may employ to identify the overall backwardness of the community. The post-independent India too continues to suffer from various problem in the development scenario inspite of the fact that growth has been registered in several sectors of the economy. The problems like poverty, unemployment, illiteracy etc., are still the priority sector in the system of governance. At the same time one would like to probe into specific problem faced by the Muslim community in general so far as the receiving of the benefits from the governmental efforts is concerned. It may be argued that due to lack of government's concern about development of the community, it remained undeveloped in comparison to other sections of society in India. There is an argument advocated by Muslims wherein the reason is attributed to the state and the system whereas others emphasize the Muslim's mentality of defeatism and motivational deficit as the reason for the backwardness. In any case, the backwardness continues and therefore, it has to be addressed in broader societal interests.

Looking from the view point of growth, the education constitutes the core concern. This is the *sine qua non* for any kind of development and therefore should be addressed first. During 1973-74 Gopal Krishna had conducted a study of Muslim's attitude and their places in Indian society. As the study was sponsored by the Ministry of Home Affairs, its findings are not available but Saxena (1983) revealed that Gopal Krishna found that educational level of Muslims is lower and dropout rate is higher in all parts of India and in every economic category. This state of backwardness of Muslims has been found to prevail even in Muslim-managed schools and colleges where there is no possibility of discrimination against them. A survey of Muslim-managed schools and college showed that there was dropout from 83.8 per cent enrolment percentage at school level to 40.4

per cent at the college level.[3] It has also been submitted that Muslims are not only educationally backward in the North, they are also backward in all parts of India. In Tamil Nadu as many as 10 associations are working for the cause of Muslim education and yet Muslims are classified as a backward class eligible for educational concessions (Ali 1989). The picture is dismal in the case of Calcutta too where Muslims constitute 15 per cent of the population out of which three-fourth live in slums. The total enrolment of Muslims in schools is 2.2 per cent and at higher level the percentage is 0.50 per cent (Siddiqui).[4] These figures illustrate the fact that there is general lack of education among Muslims and this is true for every region of the country.

Interlinked with the educational perspective, is the question of economic condition. Further, associated with the economic conditions of Muslims is their representation in Government and Quasi Government jobs. A reference of the work done by Abdul Salam (1989) is pertinent in this context he developed a qualitative index of equality (CE) based on the ratio of percentage of presentation of a community to percentage share of that community in the total population the ratio multiplied by 100 provide the coefficient of equality (CE). The departures of the CE from 100 on the lower side is an indication of backwardness of a community. The CE found for different levels of jobs in public and private sectors provides a picture of measurable conditions of Muslims employment even in class IV posts in public and private sector undertakings and state government jobs. Most of the Muslims are earning by working as electricians, mechanics, craftier and artisan. However, one finds certain island of prosperity in some towns of Uttar Pradesh (Muradabad, Aligarh, Mau, Varanasi) and Maharashtra (Bhiwandi) where Muslim entrepreneurs can be found among manufacturers and wholesale trader, in textiles, carpets, locks and brass stencils.[5] Economically, therefore, the community generally remain backward and not much by way of Government support is witnessed for improving the lot of these people.

It could be noted here that the salience regarding deprivation in social, economic and political areas among Muslims and the effect of salience of deprivation in different areas on inter-group attitudes of Muslims were studied by Tripathi and Srivastava (1979). Data collected from a sample of 112 Muslim students of Allahabad University showed that deprivation was highest in economic areas and lowest in social area. Moreover, Muslims suffering from greater feelings of deprivation were found to attribute higher negative qualities to the out-group but the difference of level of deprivation was not found to be associated with the difference in the attribution of positive qualities to the out-group.[6] The findings of this study may help us in finding explanations to the problems of economics deprivation in Muslim community.

It has also been argued that the economic profile of Muslims is varied. Traders, businessmen, merchants and industrialists are no doubt comfortably placed as mentioned earlier, but the vast majority of Muslims including the impoverished peasants and landless laboureres, are the bulk of the rural poor and the industrial proletariat.[7] It is alleged that the fortunes of Muslim professionals dwindled and their influence waned after partition, get some of them have prospered during recent decade owing to expansion of trade, economic, industry and the service sectors in medium sized urban centres, and some have benefited from powerful social and class factors, and family and political ties.[8] Some studies have been conducted to examine the nature, the cause and the implications of 'Muslim Backwardness' which help us in understanding the issue involved.

Voices have kept coming up about various aspects of Muslim Minorities in the country. On 19-20 December 1964 the *Indian Express* carried out two articles describing the positions of 55 million Muslims as 'sad'. Its author A.G. Noorani commented on the Muslim unequal treatment in employment, and on the threat to their physical security. 'Add to this a near denial of even the right to agitate for redress, even to ventilate grievances, and you have the malaise clearly spell out'. Badruddin Tayabji, a retired diplomat, stressed much the same themes four years later in three articles published in the *Statesman*.[9] Several others have contributed airing similar views. The picture emerging from such writings is familiar. A larger minority of the Muslims—nearly 71% — live in rural areas, and are mostly landless labourers, small and marginal farmers, artisans, craftsmen and shopkeepers. Their social stratification and class interests are more or less the same as those of other people in the countryside. More than half of the Muslim urban population live below the poverty line, compared to about 35 per cent Hindus.[10] This explains the difference in economic status of the community.

In view of the various problems faced by the Muslim population in the country, the present Seminar focused attention on the following areas as a sub-theme (a) Employment Scenario; (b) Socio-economic Status; and (c) General.

NOTES

1. Laura D. Jenkins, "Caste, Class and Islam: Boundaries of Backwardness in India," *The Eastern Anthropologist*, Ethnographic

& Folk Culture Society, Lucknow, Vol. 53, No. 3-4, July-December, 2000, p. 327.

2. Mushirrul Hasan, *Legacy of a Divided Nation: India's Muslim Since Independence,* Oxford University Press, New Delhi, 1997.
3. Qunar Hasan, "Life space of Indian Muslim," *Eastern Anthropologist,* Ethnographic and Folk Culture Society, Lucknow, Vol. 53, No. 3-4, July-December 2000, p. 415.
4. *Ibid.*
5. *Ibid.*, pp. 415-416.
6. *Ibid.*, p. 417.
7. Legacy of a Divided Nation, *op. cit.*, Primary Literature on the Economic Status of the Muslims is thin; so one relies on strategy and inconclusive evidence based on field survey, personal accounts and newspaper reports.
8. *Ibid.*, p. 8.
9. Badruddin Tayabji, 'Participation of Minorities in all walks of life: Minorities are an Asset not Properly Untitled: Minorities as Contributors to National Life.
10. *Legacy of a Divided Nation, op. cit.*, p. 281.

PART – I

EMPLOYMENT SCENARIO

1

MINORITY'S ISSUES AND STATE INTERVENTION: AN APPROACH WITH A DIFFERENCE

—Mohammad Haleem Khan

Vision Statement

Concern for providing safeguards to the constitutional rights of the minorities has always been the cornerstone of governance of the modern Indian state. As a concomitant to the constitutional obligation, welfare of minorities has, accordingly, been an integral part – albeit with questionable success, of the planning process and design of various development and welfare programmes and schemes. Despite the growth of the economy and the increased state intervention in the life and affairs of the citizens, the minorities have been found wanting in being able to take advantage of the various development and welfare schemes and accordingly could not contribute to the economic growth commensurate to their numbers and as laggards have been pulling down the per capita GDP growth. Any overt concern shown in this regard has often been trivialised by demagoguery — obviously, with an eye on short-term gains and for reasons of political expediency. Socio-economic context of an enlightened nation's concern for the development and welfare of its minorities, therefore, need be articulated, widely published and painstakingly imbibed in the normal course of the affairs of the state in addition to the constitutional and moral obligations:

- The constitution provides for security to life and property of minorities and therein, is enshrined the right of minorities to conserve their culture and establish and administer educational institutions of their choice.
- India, being a civilised nation and one of the important signatory of UN Charter, is morally committed to look-after its minorities.

Unfortunately, because of the political trivialization of the issue, the impression has gained ground that all talk of development and welfare of minorities is an aberration of our polity. It has not dawned on many of us that even USA – an advanced economy and no lesser a democracy, has programs broadly known as affirmative action to improve race relations – read minorities' welfare.

The harsh economic rationale of development and welfare of minorities has to be brought home to all and sundry. Indian economy after liberalization, for the first time, has been able to register growth rate and has shown depth that it has made the world look at Indian as another emerging economic giant. If Indian has to sustain its economic growth rate and measure itself at par with other newly industrializing economies of East Asia, viz., China, Malaysia, Thailand, Indonesia, etc. than it can not leave nearly one fifth of its population on the frings of economic activities and at level of subsistence. *To sustain the high growth rate, the imperatives of the economic-logic demand that no significant social and religious group of population is left out of the ongoing mobilization towards economic growth.* This is possible only when socio-economic indicators of minority community do not significantly differ from the national averages. Once this changed perspective informs the polity and is widely understood and appreciated, as the basis and rationale behind the state intervention for development and welfare of minorities, the approach and strategy will unveil itself. This vision statement and consequential paradigm shift in the design and planning of the development and welfare schemes for minorities will have to be internalized and accordingly, innovative options for their implementation will have to be thought of.

Goals and Objectives

In view of our sovereign aspirations to achieve and sustain higher rates of economic growth and also to be counted as self-propelling economic giant among the comity of nations, minorities, which constitute 18%* of the country's population, have to be empowered sufficiently so that the per capita contribution of minorities in the GDP does not pull the national averages down. An approach to minority issues, therefore, has to address the following pre-requisites—

- Security to life and property and peaceful working environment, conducive to let people pursue their vocations to excel.
- Socio-economic indicators of minorities do not significantly lag behind the national averages, and
- Cultural sensibilities do not suffer from the threat of obliteration and, therefore, mix and marinade with gay abandon for mutual regeneration, rejuvenation, cross fertilization and enrichment.

Once the goal to achieve the rapid economic growth and sustain it informs the dos and don'ts of our polity and

* As per 1991 census

the above mentioned broad objectives vis-à-vis minorities' issues gain wider currency, the approach will also acquire clarity, become generally acceptable and might even gain mass appeal in due course of time.

THE APPROACH

Time and again it has been amply brought home that the steps taken to ameliorate the socio-economic conditions of the minorities and the efforts to enhance their participation in the development process have not yielded the desired results. An *ab initio* discussion of issues involved, therefore, is a must.

The welfare scheme's impact on the target group depends on-

- the nature of schemes,
- the absorption capacity of the target group, and
- the delivery system and its reach.

The lack of desirable impact of the government efforts in improving the lot of Muslims (Muslims constitute the largest chunk of minorities) has been variously assessed (Gopal Singh Committee report, to name one). Notwithstanding some problems with the schemes like madarsa modernisation that provides one teacher to each madarsa, irrespective of the number of students, classes and subjects to be taught, it may not be easy to place blame at the door of scheme design alone and substantively.

It is equally ironical that the issue of schemes not being found popular has not been put to deeper analysis. Instead, poor performance has been glossed over by painting the minority community as closed to all external initiative because of orthodoxy and such other clinched value judgements which border on describing the minority community's behaviours as irrational – even somewhat afflicted by self-destructive Freudian logic.

Perfection in the scheme design and forward-looking attitudinal response of the minorities is of paramount importance. Lest it be misconstrued, lack of these attributes is not peculiar to minorities' welfare arena; these weaknesses, more or less, haunt all the developmental activities and all the beneficiary groups.

This paper proposes a paradigm shift in the area of delivery.

In 1835 Macaulay wrote the historic words: instead of funding of institutions providing traditional education, East India Company should deploy the resources for the development of modern education infrastructure. If one takes a charitable view, one may not find Macaulay's dictate on education bizarre. It was imperative for him to optimise the returns from the expenditure on education – the objective being to create a system that generates sufficiently trained manpower (call babus, if you like) to serve the needs of the Company. One may debate whether Macaulay could have suggested undertaking the modernisation of the traditional system rather than creation of a totally new one. Who knows, his intention to create psychological domination to prepare the ground for the ultimate colonisation might have come in the way! The modern welfare state India is, the purpose of state intervention, however, may not be conceived to be limited to fulfil the *primary* need of having sufficient trained manpower. The *secondary* benefits, namely, to unleash the economic and entrepreneurial potential of its citizens to create avenues for employment outside the government sector and to encourage manufacture and consumption of goods and services are of great consequence. The welfare state also depends heavily on the *tertiary* benefits of state intervention, that is, the synergetic implications in the area of social mobility, enrichment of equality of life, etc.

To improve the delivery of welfare schemes amongst the minority community, especially Muslims both the formal and alternative delivery systems are to be strengthened and empowered.

STEPS SUGGESTED

Empowerment of the Traditional Institutions as Alternative Delivery System

The accessibility of the governmental machinery and its limitation in reaching the benefits of the welfare schemes to masses has been widely commented upon. Of late, a lot

ETYMOLOGY	
MADARSA	*MAKATEB*
'Madarsa in Urdu is acknowledged as a word of Arabic origin and means school, college, academy e.g. 'madarsa ibtidaai' meaning primary school. The word 'daras'—a Persian noun means 'lesson, lecture'. According to the 'The Concise Persian-English Dictionary' by Abbas Aryanpur-Kashani and Manooochehr Aryanpur-Kashani, published by Amir Kabir Publication Organisation, 1990, "Madarsa" means school, academy, Lyceum institute, gymnasium, lycee	According to 'The Concise Persian-English dictionary' by Abbas Aryanpur-Kashani and Manoochehr Aryanpur-Kashani, published by Amir Kabir Publication Organisation, 1990, 'Makateb' in Persian means one-class schools, and 'Kitab' means book, Bible. In Urdu 'makateb' means a school, an academy and is known as a word of Persian origin.

Text Box 1

more role is being chalked out for institutions, commonly known as NGOs for dispensing the welfare schemes. The accessibility of the governmental agencies and their capability to reach the *minorities* in all reasonableness could not be presumed to be better. This failure though, has largely been credited to the conservatism of minorities themselves. The modern voluntary institutions, commonly referred as NGOs specialising in the area of minorities' welfare, are, but a few. Unfortunately the old Macaulay like mind-set continues to make it almost impossible to take cognisance of the long tested and time established voluntary institutions thrown up by the minority community from within. Since modern India's approach has to be different, one has to take stock of these traditional voluntary institutions as an alternative delivery system. Suitably empowered, the reach of these institutions may be harnessed in such a way that while they continue to discharge their duty by the community in the traditional sense, they also acquire enough dynamism to become vehicles of change and mature into an effective delivery system for various development and welfare schemes for the minorities.

A close and serious look into the social dynamics of the Muslim community will make it apparent that the following quasi-religious voluntary institutions have been sustaining the socio-economic fabric of the community for hundreds of years.

1. Madarsa
2. Makateb
3. Wakf including orphanages
4. Master craftsman and the vocational trainee system, and
5. The Zakaat

These institutions have used their tenacity of purpose to serve various needs of the community. Their relevance and reach has been established on the bedrock of performance.

- Dovetailing Traditional Educational Institutions to serve as the vehicles of Modern Education—

Madarsas in quintessence are a measure of voluntary efforts within the community, which highlights

1. Entrepreneurial capabilities,
2. Capacity to mobilise resources, and
3. Commitment to learning.

Only deterioration with time has been inability to modernise and to update the scope of learning. In view of the competing demands and the ultimate limitation of availability of resources, it was rightly realised that mere provisions of financial assistance for establishing more schools may not help the Muslim community much. The government of India therefore, launched scheme for the modernisation of madarsas. It envisaged supplementing the financial resources of madarsas that included learning of modern languages/ subjects, e.g., English, Hindi, science, Mathematics and socially useful productive work (SUPW) along with the traditional subjects. The scheme though laudable, in real terms means an annual financial inflow of nearly Rs. 26000/-.*

An organisation, running these *madarsas* on acres of land and having constructed tens of rooms and spending lakhs of rupees annually, may rightly not find it worthwhile to open themselves to the interference of the government

* As per relevant GOI guidelines as in 1995.

machinery and make liable the madarsa, for submission of returns and reports for the meagre sum of Rs 26,000 per year.

Unfortunately without much thought, this most rational and cost effective response of madarsa management was treated as one more example of obscurantism. This scheme, if to be implemented in the right earnest, must provide the madarsas undertaking modernisation enough where withals to meet the requirement of teachers on the basis of number of students, classes and subjects to be taught. Barring a few exceptions, most of the madarsas should be keen to modernise, provided it means so in the real terms to make their efforts worthwhile.

Traditional Education System	
MADARSA	*MAKATEB*
These are boarding schools, running on religious charity viz,... 'Zakaat', and are mostly being made use of by the children of very poor parents who value their children being educated, notwithstanding the fact that the system restricts the choice to religious instructions only.	These are day schools paid for by the local community to initiate their wards into basics of religion i.e.., being able to read the Book, say prayers etc... But for the comparatively rich, even the girl child attends these institutions which initiate them into letters, albeit Arabic.

Text Box 2

Madarsas certificates need be declared equivalent to high school and secondary board certificates. Madarsas that are providing facilities for graduate and postgraduate studies similarly be made eligible for affiliation with the universities in relevant subjects.

Most of the alumni of madarsas ultimately become Imams in the mosques. Pesh-imamat at best is an underemployment situation. It is the need of the hour that the would-be-Imams are additionally given some vocational training and made computer literate so that in between leading prayers, they could use their spare time in some manufacturing activity, work as data entry operators, do desk top publishing, etc. Understandably, Urdu computers are available, madarsas imparting the high school and secondary level learning be, therefore, covered under vocational training and computer literacy programmes of the government made available to such institutions running *madarsas* and that are on voluntary of India. It has more chances to succeed in *madarsas* then in formal school system that was historically designed to produce clerks for the then East India Company.

Some of the *madarsa* institutions have shown rare entrepreneurial capabilities, both in terms of management as well as resources mobilisation. Once these *madarsas* are recognised as alternative delivery institutions for the propagation of education and vocational training, some of these madarsa institutions gathering courage and confidence in governmental support will be able to start ITIs and polytechnics too. The *madarsas*, therefore, can be the nucleus and the *madarsa* management may provide the much sought after private initiative for the propagation of education amongst Muslims. Mini-ITI schemes under which Rs. 10* lakhs are provided for establishing a mini-ITI as one time grant should be made available to such institutions running Madarsas and that are on voluntary basis, willing to start vocational course and acquire the status of a mini-ITI.

To sum up, a serious attempt will have to be made to do away with the so-called mischief of Macaulay's famous dictate of 1835. Traditional educational institutions; namely, *madarsas* and makatebs are to be empowered to become

---

* As per relevant GOI guidelines as in 1996.

vehicles of modern education along with their traditional role. *The present scheme of modernisation of madarsas is, at best symbolic.* The scheme for modernisation of madarsas has to be broad-based. *Madarsas* that opt for modernisation need be supported with

- **Sufficient number of teachers for teaching Science, Maths, English, and Hindi, at the rate of one teacher for 40 students,**
- Help in developing suitable syllabus and reading/ teaching materials,
- Coverage of madarsas under the 'vocational education scheme for +2 level schools',
- Coverage of madarsas under the computer literacy programme, and
- Enabling well-managed Madarsas to run vocational courses and acquire the status of mini ITIs.

Makateb 'SWOT' Analysed	
Strengths	*Opportunities*
• Represent the community's commitment to a minimum level of universal learning; • Are the proof of community's universal capacity to organise and manage elementary learning institutions; • ability to find wherewithal; • a self supporting non gove-rnmental organisation (NGO); • acceptability as a place of basic learning; and • reach in the community.	• As an NGO, to supplement the formal delivery system of the state to enthuse the community towards modern concerns of a welfare state; • Empower the children with the choice to switch over the modern education; • Proliferation of education for all; and • Supervision being local, the implied finality must result in much responsible teacher behaviour.

Makatebs are the other important traditional educational institutions. These provide for the basic need of universal religious instructions. Unfortunately, it has been internalized by the community for dubious reasons that since they will not be able to garner government jobs, there is little purpose of costly mainstream education (Somehow the myth 'the purpose of education is to get a government job' has not only survived but also has been supplemented with the other myth, namely, the government is the largest and the best source of employment). Makatebs have unique strengths. These are the only institutions where Muslim girl child also goes for education, that is, initiation in basic religious teachings. If Muslim girl child's education is to be addressed and she is to be empowered it may to be attempted through these institutions that have wider acceptability as well as accessibility amongst Muslims. A

Weakness	*Threats*
• Being funded from voluntary contribution by the local community, on *equitable* basis, has poor resource *elasticity;* • Scarceness of resources; • Limited expectation of the stakeholders and narrowly defined rule; and • Micro organisation.	• Mechanism of supervision will have to be sensitized to develop empathy with the system; • Long term and consistent use of resources invested; and • Too clearly demarcated end use of resources may be difficult to be attempted

Text Box 3

few of these institutions have been recognised on a year-to-year basis, as primary schools in U.P. Makatebs can ideally be the home for non-formal education centres. If 20% of a state's NFE centres are earmarked and made to run from the Makatebs, it will immensely help reaching the modern education to Muslim girl child.

Employment of Wakfs as Modern NGOs and Amendment of the Wakf Act to Give the Wakf Boards a Truly Perpetual Character

Wakfs are the voluntary institutions whose objectives have been laid down in the Wakf deed and to fulfil those objectives certain income generating assets have been attached, so that the socio-religious objectives could be fulfilled year after year. Because of lack of renewal, with the passage of time, income generating capacity of these assets has declined and the performance of the objectives being no more possible with the meagre income, the objectives themselves have been forgotten. Present situation is so confused and off the mark that any discussion on wakf is deemed complete once it has been discussed that how costly properties are lying under-utilised because they are wakf and can not be sold legally; or with the breast beating noise on how they are being sold surreptitiously with the connivance of mutawallies (the trustees). Wakf as a non-governmental organisation catering to certain socio-religious (broadly speaking charitable) objectives is not topical for discussion. The wakf Act 1995 has been promulgated and notified. Institutional arrangements at the state level and the Central Wakf act 1995 has been promulgated and notified. Institutional arrangements at the state level and the Central Wakf council need be strengthened and invigorated. The efficacy of the scheme of things has to be judged on the basis as to how much extra income has been generated from the wakf properties and what social, charitable, religious objectives could be fulfilled. Even in the present condition, some of the properties could be used for running schools and *Anganwadi Kendras.* Wakf properties, being mostly located in the heart of the Muslim locality, will provide an ideal backdrop for launching developmental schemes.

Central Wakf Council needs financial strengthening and should be reorganised and developed on the lines of CAPART, as an agency for implementing various developmental schemes through wakfs; wakfs and wakf boards performing roles akin to NGOs.

Under the Wakf Act, 1995, like in the erstwhile dispensation, the Wakf Boards are purported to have a life of five years, after which fresh elections are to be held for various categories of members and new board is to be notified thereafter. *This provision need be amended on the lines of the provisions under the company law, whereby 1/3 of the members of the board retire biannually*. This will make the new members well acquainted with the niceties of their responsibilities, will sensitize them and will also provide for consistency and smooth change over.

It should also be provided that once the election has been notified, it will be allowed to complete and elected member, pending judicial review, if any, will hold office till the election is declared null and void by the competent court. Any vacancy in the board or litigation thus will not affect the working of the Wakf Boards, which presently are mired into self-immobilizing litigation.

- **Help the Traditional Charity Flow into Religiously Compatible and Socially Desirable but Financially Starved Activities –**

All Muslims who have liquid assets beyond a prescribed limit are under religious obligation to spare and part with 2.5% of the value of these liquid assets by way of Zakaat. As per 1991 census, India has more than 10 corers Muslims. Presuming a family size of 5 to 7 persons one can visualise 1.5 to 2 corers Muslim families living in the country. Again, presuming that only 1% Muslim families fall in the categories of Zakaat-paying families, the number of Zakaat payees will be around 1.5 to 2 lakhs. Taking the average Zakaat amount to be Rs. 1000/- per family – Zakaat pool is parenting 15 crores to 20 crores every year. At present this amount gets evaporated into activities, which as per the Islamic doctrine could be undertaken from the Zakaat. Certainly, it would raise a lot hue and cry if any overt attempt were made by the government to channel it into a set of activities and is open to the criticism as under interference in the Muslim religious practices. Zakaat, given to legal entities that observe certain accountings and audit practices and run institutions like—orphanages, old age homes, destitute women and child centres and such other activities which have sanction under the Islamic Law and also serve a modern society's needs, if made income tax exempt, good amount of money (as shown above 15 to 10 corers) can be made available to these socially relevant sectors. It will also have some positive,. confidence building effect upon the community as it will be able to rediscover itself as a community that is able to mobilise resources of its own and run socially relevant modern institutions on the pattern of much envied Christian missions. The majority community will also develop a better perception of the Muslim community and its religious practices in view of these much more visible socially relevant ventures.

PRIME MINISTER'S 15-POINT PROGRAMME FOR WELFARE OF MINORITIES

Out of her concern for the welfare of the minorities, the then Prime Minister, Smt. Indira Gandhi addressed a letter to the Chief Ministers in May 1983 containing certain points to ensure the economic, social and educational development of minorities. This letter covered 15 different aspects for action commonly known as the Prime Minister's 15-Point Programme for Welfare of the Minorities. These points were retained by Prime Minister, Shri Rajiv Gandhi in his letter dated 28th August 1985 addressed to all the Chief Ministers. The text of these points is given below.

I. Communal Riots

1. In the areas, which have been identified as communally sensitive and riot prone District and Police Officials of the highest known efficiency, impartiality and secular record must be posted. In such areas and even elsewhere, the prevention of communal tension should be one of the primary duties of DM, and SP. Their performances in this regard should be an important factor in determining their promotion prospects.
2. Good work done in this regard by District and Police Officials should be rewarded.
3. Severe action should be taken against all those who incite communal tensions or take part in violence.
4. Special court or courts specifically earmarked to try communal offences should be set up so that offenders are brought to book speedily.
5. Victims of communal riots should be given immediate relief and provided prompt and adequate financial assistance for their rehabilitation.
6. Radio & TV must also help in restoring confidence, communal harmony and peace in such affected areas.
7. It is unfortunate that certain sections of the Press sometimes indulge in tendentious reporting and publication of objectionable and inflammatory material, which may incite communal tension. Editors, printers, publishers and other concerned will cooperate in finding a way to avoid publication of such material.

II. Recruitment to State and Central Services

8. In the recruitment of police personnel State Governments should be advised to give special considerations to minorities. For this purpose, the composition of Selection Committees should be representative.
9. The Central Government should take similar action in the recruitment of personnel to the Central Police Forces.
10. Large scale employment opportunities are provided by the Railways, Nationalized Banks and Public Sector Enterprises. In these cases also the concerned departments should ensure that special consideration is given to recruitment from minority communities.

11. In many areas recruitment is done through competitive examinations. Often minority groups have been handicapped in taking advantage of the educational system to compete on equal terms in such examinations. To help them to overcome these handicaps steps should be to encourage the starting of coaching classes in minority educational institutions to train persons to complete successfully in these examinations.
12. The acquisition of technical skills by those minorities who are today lagging behind would also help in national development. Arrangements should be made to set up it and polytechnics by Government or private agencies in predominantly minority areas to encourage admission in such institutions of adequate number of persons belonging to these communities.

III. Other Measures

13. In various development programmes including the 20-Point Programme, care should be taken to see that minorities secure in a fair and adequate measure the benefits flowing there from. In the various communities, which are set to oversee the implementation of such programmes, members of these communities should be actively involved.
14. Apart from the above general issues there are various local problems, which develop into needless irritants to minorities. For instance encroachment of wakf properties and on graveyards have led to protests and grievances in some places. Suitable steps should be taken to deal with such problems on an expeditious and satisfactory basis.
15. Problems relating to minorities need to be attended to on a continuing basis so that apprehensions are allayed and genuine grievances redressed. To facilitate this, a special cell will be created in the Ministry of Home Affairs to deal with matters relating to minorities.

Text Box 4

- **Making the Prime Minister's 15 Point Programme for Minorities Operational (see Text Box 4)**

Though the Prime Minister's 15-point programme for welfare of minorities is an well-articulated dossier of intentions, it is yet to be converted into specific schemes and programmes and result into clearly defined procedures and systems to make its impact being felt at the ground level. Following areas / points need specific system based support mechanism to ensure commitments getting converted into acts.

Points No. 1 & 2

Though the D.Ms & S.Ps have been assigned the prevention of communal tension as primary duty yet riots have taken place and may continue to take place. Wherever riots have taken place-

* Either the commissions of inquiry have not finalised their reports, or
* Their recommendations have not been followed up/ acted upon.

It is therefore, suggested that a law be enacted to provide for the commission of inquiries being setup in all cases of communal riots fulfilling given criteria or otherwise, if the government is so satisfied. The legislation must also provide for fixation of tenure and terms of reference of the commission and procedure for extension thereof and making its recommendation obligatory to be implemented according to a time bound fixed schedule; of course, the house will have the residuary powers to return the recommendations of the commission for fresh probe etc.

Point No. 3

A provision in the rules of business must be incorporated to inform the house, say during the budget session about the action taken against elements inciting communal tension.

Pint No. 4

Though the special courts have been set up / designated

to try the communal offences, yet the cases mostly get converted into a long drawn protracted litigation with no end. A time limit has to be fixed for the conclusion of the cases in the trial courts and suitable mechanism has to be developed to ensure that the High Courts are much more conscious of pursuing the timely disposal of these cases.

Point No. 5

On the line of the Workmen Compensation Act, suitable legislation is overdue to provide for obligatory and timely financial help and rehabilitation of communal riot victims. The transparency thus brought about into the calculation and fixation of the compensation amount will go a long way in reposing the faith in the government's sensitivity in such matters.

Points No. 6 & 7

A body on the pattern of 'Lok Ayukt' for prevention of corruption' and 'Press council of India for making media accountable' need be constituted under a status with adjudicatory powers [its pronouncements having the force of the verdict of a High Court]. The media reporting and public speeches / pronouncements could be scrutinised / analysed by this statutory body and erring press correspondents and public representatives could be made answerable / accountable for inciting communal tension.

Points No. 8, 9, 10 & 11

For the recruitment and ensuring a fair representation of minorities in State Police / Central Police, railways, Banks and Public Enterprises authorities have been exhorted to give 'special consideration' to minorities. This 'special consideration' phrase is yet to be defined in concrete dos and don'ts to make any dent into the woefully negligible representation of minorities in the services. This dispensation has not made much headway because it is yet to be understood as a measure that will make the police much more credible institution – the need of a modern police force. Like trivialisations of all types, this has also been primarily perceived as a play to give jobs to Muslims.

Point No. 12

To encourage minorities to set up technical institutions in the private sector, in the Muslim concentration blocks, mini-ITI scheme of the Rural Development ministry is additionally implemented through minority institutions.

It will be worthwhile to have a scheme to provide some financial assistance to ITI's and polytechnics being set up by the minority institutions. Even if the grant is notional, it will generate promotional thrust and also take away from the minorities the so-called self-internalised perception that even if they try to establish such institutions, they may not get through the maze of official approvals etc.

- **Creation of a Parliamentary Committee for the Supervision of effectiveness of Programmes and Schemes for the Minorities and also the participation of these communities in the development scheme in general.**

It has generally been accepted by all sections of society that the Indian constitution is one of most progressive and modern constitution, which amply provides for the well being of all sections of the society. State policy and programmes have also been seldom found inherently wanting in their sweep, so as to benefit selectively. It is, however, an accepted fact that all sections of the society have not been able to take advantage of the welfare measures. The benefits of the development have not percolated down uniformly – minorities as a group has, somehow, got sidelined and their participation in the developmental activities has been abysmally low. Governments have, accordingly, constituted various commission and committees in the past to recommend suitable measures; like, 'Three Language Formula', Kothari Commission in the area of education, and enactments like the Wakf Act, to name a few. State government has variously implemented the recommendations of these commissions and committees. The implementation of the Wakf Act has also been lackadaisical. This has caused a lot of heartburn and disillusionment. In certain sections of minorities governmental welfare measures have been perceived more as lip service. Mostly, this can be accounted for in terms of lack of empathy on the part of delivery system and absence of a strong institutional mechanism enforcing accountability and answerability. It is, therefore, suggested that a *Parliamentary Committee for National Integration and Minority Issues,* on the lines of Public Accounts Committee, be instituted so that the implementing agencies can be made answerable in a much more direct way. Similarly, Legislative Committees need be created at the state level. The proposed Parliamentary Committee for National Integration and minority issues and the respective Legislative Committees will be obliged to submit their reports annually before the house during the budget session.

- **Deepening the Efforts to Strengthen Economic Activities among Minorities**

These efforts can be generally summed up in terms of measures to improve availability of capital. Creation of National Minority Development and Finance Corporation (NMDFC) has been rightly described as landmark beginning Present state financial endowments and avenues for future replenishment of capital of NMDFC as well as the state channeling agencies, however, do not inspire confidence in their long-term sustainability. Presently, sources of fund of NMDFC are restricted to 25% equity capital contribution from the central government and 75% equity contribution from the state governments. The poor financial health of the state governments further erodes the confidence in the sustained availability of resources with the NMDFC Presuming that for legal reasons the central government has to be a minority shareholder in the NMDFC, its share could easily be enhanced to 49%.

Similarly, state-channeling agencies (the State Minority Financial and Development Corporations – SMFDCs) should also be strengthened by 49% contribution in their equity capital by the central government.

Having conceded the above imperatives of strengthening the equity capital structure of NMDFC and broad-basing the equity capital of state channeling agencies, the role of these institutions can be made effective and sustainable only if the NMDFC is empowered and sources of its funds augmented beyond the equity contribution from the state and central Governments. NMDFC will have to be empowered on the lines of IDBI, SIDBI, and NABARD so as to be able to borrow from multilateral agencies; both IDA and loans as well as resort to commercial borrowing from the domestic market. NMDFC's scale of activities too will have to be defined in the perspective, as to what amount-per-capita-minority-population is to be channeled in a span of a plan period so as to create a given number of self employment ventures and associated employment opportunities.

- **Overhaul of the Education related Regulations – both Central and State**

Most of the regulations governing the opening of new

educational institutions, award of the affiliation with an examining body, grant of permission to start new subjects/ trades etc., are absolute, archaic and are of the genre whereby the state intervention in the affairs-education in the name of maintaining the quality of education was nothing but the means by any other name to fulfil the self serving need of the education bureaucracy. The spirit of liberalization of economy and 'the mechanics of competition being the guarantee of quality' is yet to inform the education administration. The result is – declining standards of education, inadequacy of educational infrastructure, burgeoning queues for admission, evaporation of private capital from education etc. Whenever there is a big gap between demand and supply of any facility, as we know, not only the corruption and decline in the standards take place, but also, the deprived sections of the society suffer the most leading to enhancement of inequities. Gopal Singh Committee has clearly brought out that Muslims and neo-Buddhists are the most educationally backward. In the above scenario of strong state controlled education regime, Muslims, being also other wise confused about their educational priorities, have become the biggest losers. If the *education for* all thrust is to translate into reality, then opening of schools etc. has to be fully deregulated. Affiliation of an examination body should be optional, like ISI mark. It will go a long way to promote education and also to increase the availability of educational infrastructure if all regulations are scrapped that inhibit private participation. The private enterprise be given a free hand to open and run schools that also get closed if they are found to be lacking in quality by the sheer force of lack of demand. To help standarisation, an *Education Authority* may be created which on the pattern of awarding star-status for hotels and export houses, will categorize educational institutions, depending upon the availability of building, laboratories, play ground, quality and quantity of teaching faculty and previous year's performance. The schools may even be granted freedom to prepare students for whatever examining body they prefer. Some schools might become so prestigious, over a period of time that their internal examination itself becomes a measure of excellence. A *comprehensive overhaul of various education regulations with a thrust towards deregulation will go a long way in helping the minorities along with others in establishing educational institutions and managing them as per the enlightened spirit and loftiest ideals enshrined in our constitution.*

- **Publication of Census and NSS Socio-economic Data—communitywise**

There is a severe lack of reliable data on the socio-economic conditions of minorities. This results in minority community internalising subjectively, the feeling that the state is not concerned about their deteriorating socio-economic condition; at the same time any governmental intervention to improve the lot of minorities is trivialised as a vote catching device. Like population, socio-economic data be published communitywise — both in the census and relevant national sample survey (NSS) so that the socio-economic rationale of governmental intervention to help minorities, could be understood by citizens of the country in the proper perspective. The data will help in the formulation of suitable strategy. Programmes and schemes could also be, accordingly, tailor-made.

- **Sensitisation of the Delivery System**

It has been sufficiently given importance in the 15-point programme of the Prime Minister for the minorities that concerted monitoring from the district to state level and the Prime Minister's Office is required to make the programs reach the minorities. In view of the fact that this stipulation has been there since 1983, and desirable results are yet to materialise. It is proposed that in all states where minority population is 8% or above a separate department under a full-fledged secretary to the state government be created which will not only administer the specific schemes relating to minority but also, by active liaison and co-ordination, ensures that minorities participate fully, in developmental schemes being implemented by various government departments.

Similarly, state governments shall create a district level minority welfare office establishment in all districts where the minority population is 8% or above. For some sparsely populated districts this percentage may be converted into a cut-off minimum population.

The Government of India may, in the ministry of welfare, create a separate minority cell headed by an additional secretary to Government of India who will not only be responsible for schemes and programmes of the ministry but also for coordination with other ministries with a view to enhance their participation.

Creation of an independent department at the State Government level and district level office, though necessary, may it self not be sufficient. The general developmental machinery being exposed to the trivialization of various development measures, especially those relating to minorities, as vote catching devices in the press as well as during the heat of political process, have to be given orientation training capsules – both at the time of induction training and then as refresher courses at a gap of 10 years. The training should cover all field functionaries, Block Development Officers, Police Inspectors, Tehsildars and various *State civil services* so that the socio-economic imperatives of the minority welfare and related development schemes are not lost upon them.

- **Participation of Minorities in the Governance**

Under the 15-point programme of the Prime Minister the representation of minority in various government, quasi-government departments and public undertaking is monitored. For improving their share in the recruitment, a Muslim member's presence in the interview/recruitment board has been repeatedly emphasised. Understandably, the purpose of having a fair number of minority employees is not limited to just giving jobs to many more Muslims. This, probably, has also been found desirable as it-

- Provides the community a sense of participation in the governance of the country,
- Enhances synergy with development activities,
- Works as a catalyst for social mobility, and
- If the system of spoils is presumed to be working, the community is additionally benefited.

In states where majority of the minority community resides, percentage of government servants belonging to minorities hovers around 2 to 6 per cent. Given all the commitment, short of the reservation of jobs for the minorities, bringing this percentage anywhere near their share in population is bound to take a lot of time. The State Governments may, therefore, be advised that in view of the above-mentioned ramifications, the available employees belonging to minority communities be, as far as possible, posted in the districts that have been identified as minority concentration districts.

Education of Muslim Girls

Minorities being otherwise lagging behind in terms of

Human Development Index, the socio-economic condition of women and girls is bound to be much worse. To make a tangible dent, special dispensation will have to be made. It is proposed that Muslims (identified) the most educationally backward by the Gopal Singh Committee report) be encouraged to open one girls high school in the private sector in each Muslim concentration block and one inter college for girls at all the district headquarters, of course, other communities will be able to avail of the facility. In cases where no Muslim *anjuman* comes forward, the organisation / societies running the madarsas be roped in. This has to be liberally funded to supplement the poor resource base of the community.

SUMMING UP

The country is at the crossroads of developments of historical significance. In the worldwide scenario of liberalization and globalization even the importance of national boundaries has been made subservient to the tidal waves of economic upheavals. The Indian nation with its continental size and minority population of country-like-magnitude can not afford the luxury of letting the vast population of minorities lie low as sleeping partners. They have to be empowered, assimilated and made a wholehearted participant in the gamut of economic activities. The challenge before our polity and its policy planners in designing measures targeted at a well defined religious, social, or an otherwise deprived section of group of people is, therefore, twofold:

- Articulation and publicity of the concerns underlying the narrowly targeted state interventions in terms of larger national concerns on which there is unanimity across the length and breadth of the political spectrum so that the state interventions could be explained convincingly and are perceived as such by people at large as a 'win-win situation' and,

- The mode of delivery is so improvised as to inclusive of and which harnesses the access of traditional institutions thrown from the community that are well known for their reach in the community and those that have sustained themselves over a long period even without governmental support.

The country has been a bystander to the industrial revolution with consequential poverty and untold misery brought upon the descendants of the magnificent civilization and the great people, India and Indians are. We cannot afford to let the economic revolution knocking the doors of the 3rd millennium bypass us.

2

RESERVATION FOR MUSLIMS: A NEED OF HOUR

— Saleem Akhtar & Nafees Ahmad

Introduction

The synchronization of all the juridical, social, economical and cultural thoughts represented by the best intellectuals proclivities across the globe make sound case for "the entitlements" which are inalienable, immemorial, invioble and inherent in humble human nature. These entitlements are nothing but social, political, economic, cultural, legal, moral and ethical "claims" asked for by the individuals against the tyrannies and democracies since the inception of nation — state concept. These strivings spearheaded innumerable movements for the accomplishment and realization of an equitable New World Human Order wedded to equality, liberty, fraternity, rule of law and justice. These "natural claims" are addressed in modern international lingua franca as "human rights".

Thus the reservation policy of the government of India is based on the principles of substantive equality heading from equalitarianism to egalitarianism so that noble goals of social and gender justice could be achieved as per constitutional mandate. But discrimination still persists in its most mawkish manifestation in Indian civil society.

Any form of discrimination whether based on caste, creed, colour, race, and sex or social origin result in deprivation. Deprivation in any form does not have caste, colour or race, it is same everywhere, it is the human sufferings and wants which born out of deprivation. Thus this paper makes an attempt to re examine the pros and cons of reservation policy in this perspective.

To secure a deprivation and discrimination free society Constitution of India endeavours to secure to all its citizens – justice, liberty and fraternity. These are the foundations on which pillars of Sovereign, Socialist, Secular and Democratic Republic of India rest. Men are born equal and in order to make the right to equality meaningful and purposeful, the founding father's of the Constitution made a number of provisions to ameliorate the socio-economic conditions of backward classes besides SC and ST so as to bring them to a level comparable with the advanced sections of our society.

Thus, reservation policy is devised for social reconstruction, to build a casteless and classless society, to eliminate existing inequalities by positive measures. Articles 14, 15,16 of our Constitution provide comprehensive brolly of equality. On the other hand, Supreme Court has handed down a series of landmark judgments in relation to social justice by interpreting the Constitution.

After the Mandal Case, providing 27% reservation in the central services and public sector undertakings to the backward classes as per the recommendations of the Mandal Commission Report has created tension between Meritarian and Compensatory Principles. The recent political extension of policy of reservation at the central level for the first time has generated a lot of tensions and controversies.

Concept and Development Minorities

It is very important to understand the distinction and the relation between 'the human rights' and 'the rights of minorities', specially in the context of India, where a large number of people have been expressing doubts regarding the validity of 'minority rights' as separate from the 'human rights' in general. This, perhaps is also the reason why a State like Maharashtra after abolishing the State Commission for Minorities, has appointed the State Commission for Human Rights. This shows that there are people in this country who fail to understand minority rights; it would be in order to make some observations on this whole issue of the relationship between these sets of rights.

The first point about the 'human rights', we need to remember is that historically these came into being from the experiences of the people of the Northern Countries (Western). The historical developments of the human rights possibly can be divided into three stages, which cover a period of more than a century. The first stage begins with the bourgeois revolutions, particularly the French and American. One of the main demands at this stage was that the State should not impose any restriction on the sharing of information. The second stage of human rights development took place with the socialist revolution, during the first quarter of the twentieth century in countries like Mexico and Russia. The main focus and emphasis during the second stage was on economic, social and cultural rights of the people and the development of human rights began during the second quarter of the twentieth century with the anti-colonialist revolutions, with the stress on national self-determination and non-discrimination[1]. Because of the historical relationship of human rights with the revolutions in the Western countries we find that the United

Nations 'Universal Declaration of Human Rights (1948)' is more individualistic in nature than collectivistics.

The scope of human rights, internationally, is determined by the United Nations, through a Declaration on 10 December 1948. The purposes and principles of this Charter, according to Article 3, are to promote and encourage respect for human rights 'for all without distinction as to race, sex, language, or religion'. For implementing this international cooperation is sought, which implies that national borders put no limits to human rights, but that by their nature human rights represent trans boundary values'.[2] But thanks to some of the later major instruments of international law, actually a new system of human rights has been introduced and the rights of the minorities recognized. The best example of such an instrument is the United Nations 'Covenant on Civil and Political Rights' adopted on 16 December 1966, which came into force on 23 March 1976. In its Article 27 it says: 'In those states in which ethnic, religious or linguistic minorities exist, persons belonging to such minorities shall not be denied the right, in community with the other members of their group, to enjoy their own culture, to profess and practice their own religion, or to use their own language'.

The other important international instruments, which focused specially on the rights of minorities include: Convention on the Prevention and Punishment of the Crime of Genocide (1948), International Convention on the Elimination of All Forms of Racial Discrimination (1965); Declaration on the Elimination of all forms of Intolerance and Discrimination Based on Religion or Belief (1981) and Declaration on the Rights of Persons belonging to National or Ethnic, Religious and Linguistic Minorities (1992). The Declaration of 1992 has cleared the earlier doubts and expanded the scope of minorities' rights. In Article 1, it directs the member State concerning full protection of minorities, identity, which reads as:

Article 1:

1. State shall protect the existence of national or ethnic, cultural, religious and linguistic minorities within their respective territories, and shall encourage the promotion of that identity.
2. State shall adopt appropriate legislative and other measures to achieve those ends.[3]
3. Article 3(1) of the Declaration says: 'Persons belonging to minorities may exercise their rights including those set forth in this Declaration individually as well as in community with other members of their groups, without any discrimination'. Here in this article, individual and collective rights as a special category, has even been accepted in a 'Manual on Human Rights Reporting' of United Nations, which says.

...human rights are formulated in a way that makes the individual human being the main beneficiary.... some human rights combine individual and collective aspects. For instance, freedom to manifest religion or belief can be exercised either individual or in a community with others ... But there are also rights which by their very nature and their subject are rights of large collectivities. Cases in point are the rights of minorities, comprising considerable number of persons with common ethnic, religious or linguistic ties as well as people's rights. The latter includes the rights to self-determination, the right to development, the rights to peace and security, and the right to a healthy environment.[4]

Besides recognizing both individual and collective rights,

the Declaration of 1992 in Article 4, also has directed the member States about the protection of the human rights and fundamental freedoms of the minorities by saying 'Persons belonging to minorities may exercise fully and effectively all their human rights and fundamental freedoms without any discrimination and full equality before the law'. So as it stands today, 'minority rights' are enjoying a special status along with the human rights in general. Here it is necessary to point out that though initially the United Nations did not offer a very clear-cut mandate for the protection of minorities, yet it created an instrument in the very begining of its inception in 1947, a 'Sub-Commission on Prevention of Discrimination and Protection of minorities' to look after the needs of minorities.

Internationally, this was the status of the relationship between human rights and Minority rights, for more than four decades to accept the reality of minorities, specially of religious and linguistic minorities? May be it was, because, originally, human rights were the product of the historical context of the Western countries, which were far less pluralistic in nature. But now as the reality of pluralism has entered their contexts also, possibly its pressure has made this change easy.

On the other hand, in a country like ours, which has always been multi-religious, multi-linguistic, multi-cultural and multi-racial in nature, there was no hinderance in accepting this reality right from the time of our independence. This is the reason why our Constitution has accepted fully the principle of 'Unity in Diversity' or 'pluralism in togetherness'. About the close relationship between human rights and minority rights, this fact positively has been accepted in the protection of Human Rights Act, 1993, which also deals with constitution of the

National Commission, and the Chairperson of the National Commission for Minorities, according to Section 3 of the above Act is one of the ex-officio members along with the Chairpersons of other two national commission for the Scheduled Castes and Scheduled Tribes, and Women. Clause 3 of Section 3 of the Act has also given the reason for this ex-officio membership; it says; 'for the discharge of functions specified in clause (b) to (j) of Section 12'. These functions are to:

(b) intervene in any proceedings involving any allegation of violation of human rights pending before a court with the approval of such court.

(c) visit, under intimation to the State Government, any jail or any other institution under the control of the State Government, where persons are detained or lodged for purposes of treatment, reformation or protection to study the living conditions of the inmates and make recommendations therein;

(d) review the safeguards provided by or under the constitution or any law for the time being in force for the protection of human rights and recommend measures for their effective implementation;

(e) review the factors, including acts of terrorism that inhibit the enjoyment of human rights and recommend appropriate remedial measures;

(f) study treaties and other international instruments on human rights and make recommendations for their effective implementation;

(g) undertake and promote research in the field of human rights.

(h) Spread human rights literacy among various

sections of society and promote awareness of the safeguards available for the protection of these rights through publication, the media, seminars and other available means;

(i) encourage the efforts of non-governmental organizations and institutions working in the field of human rights.

(j) such other functions as it may consider necessary for the promotion of human rights.[5]

Among these functions- (b) to (j)- are included all the functions of the National Commission for Human Rights, except function (a), which deals with the petitions relating to the violation of human rights and negligence, in the prevention of such violation of a public servant. The role of the Chairperson of the National Commission for Minorities as ex-officio member becomes very important, because it appears that the Protection of Human Rights Act 1993 expects from him or her to discharge his or her duty in carrying on the above functions, to see that the human rights of the minorities are protected.

Right of the Minorities

The Indian Constitution makers took cognizance of the need to protect human rights, in general, and rights of minorities, in particular and incorporated articles in to Constitution to protect the same. In fact, much of what is being formulated by United Nations regarding the rights of persons belonging to national or ethnic, religious and linguistic minorities through its Charters, convenience and declarations, has already been taken care of in our Constitution. Here it may be helpful to refer to an analysis based report on the New Approaches to Minority protection' of Asbjorn Eide. Eide in his introductory statement to his suggested approaches says:

A human rights-based approach in pluralist societies must combine efforts to ensure equality in the common domain with acceptance of diversity in the separate domain. The separate domain is that reserved to the minority or its members to protect its identity as a group...the 'Common domain' includes all other aspects of social life, which are subject to regulation, by the authorities.[6]

The distinction between 'common domain' and 'separate domain' and their combination has been well maintained and protected in our Constitution. The Constitution is very clear in its preamble that the overall goal of India as a Sovereign Socialist Secular Democratic Republic is 'to secure to all its citizens: justice, social, economic and political, liberty of thought, expression, belief, faith and worship; equality of status and of opportunity; and to promote among them all fraternity assuring the dignity of the individual and the unity and integrity of the Nation[7]. In order to achieve this goal, first, the Constitution has made provision for the fundamental rights in part-III, which are justifiable and which the State has to safeguard, secondly there is another set of rights, embodied Part IV, which are connected with the social and economic rights of the people, and are known as the 'Directive Principles of State Policy.' These are not legally binding upon the state, but are 'fundamental in the governance of the country and it shall be the duty of the State to apply these principles in making laws' (Article-36). Then there is part IVA of the constitution, which spells out the fundamental duties of the Indian citizen. We do not often refer to this part, but it is equally important like Parts III and IV of fundamental rights, because this part spells out the roll of all the citizens in fulfilling the goals set in the Preamble of our Constitution. It is also important from the perspective of the minority rights. For example, a fundamental duty stated in clause (e) and (f) of Article 51 a reads:

I shall be the duty of every citizen of India.

(e) to promote harmony and the spirit of common brother hood amongst all the people of India transcending religion, linguistic and regional or sectional diversity; to renounce practices derogatory to the dignity of women;

(f) to value and preserve the rich heritage of our composite culture.[8]

Besides recognizing the truth of 'the rich heritage of our composite culture, 'our Constitution has fully provided a definite space in the Constitution for both the 'domain', i.e. 'common' as well as 'separate.'

In part III of the Constitution, which deals with the fundamental rights, it has divided these rights very clearly into two parts – The rights, which fall in the 'common domain', and the rights, which fall in the 'separate domain'. It should also be remembered that almost all the human rights covered in United Nations Universal Declaration of Human Rights of 1948 are covered in the fundamental rights 'list of our Constitution. Listed below are some such rights, which are common to both the Constitution and the Declaration.

Through Article 14 our Constitution provides for equality before the law. The same right is covered in Article 7 Universal Declaration of Human Rights.

Article 15 guarantees prohibition of discrimination on grounds of religion, race, caste, sex, or place of birth, which is dealt with in Article 2 of the Universal Declaration.

Article 16 guarantees equality of opportunity in matters of public employment, which in the Universal Declaration is dealt in Article 23.

Article 19 of both the documents guarantees protection of certain rights regarding speech, expression, etc.

Article 20 of the Constitution and Article 10 of the Declaration guarantee protection in respect of conviction for offences.

In the Constitution Article 21 deals with protection of life and personal liberty, while in the Universal Declaration it is dealt with in Article 3.

Article 22 guarantees protection against arrest and detention in certain cases, which in the Universal Declaration is dealt with in Article 11.

Article 23 of the Constitution prohibits traffic in human beings and forced labour; in the Universal Declaration all forms of slavery or servitude are prohibited in Article 4.

Article 24: Prohibition of employment of children in factories etc. There is no equivalent Article of right in the Universal Declaration.

Article 25 deals with the freedom of conscience and free profession, practice and propagation of religion; which in the Universal Declaration is deal with in Article 18.

Article 26: Freedom to manage religious affairs. There is no equivalent Article of right in the Universal Declaration.

Article 27: Freedom as to payment of taxes for promotion of any particular religion. There is no equivalent Article of right in the Universal Declaration.

Article 28: Freedom as to attendance at religious instruction or religious worship in certain educational institutions. There is no equivalent Article of right in the Universal Declaration.[9]

The rights mentioned above are the ones that come under the 'common domain'. Now for a look at the two different kinds of minority rights, which fall in the 'separate domain'. The first such right is meant for all the citizens, who form minorities in different parts of the country and the protection of their interest are guaranteed in Article – 29, which read as:

Article 29: Any section of the citizens residing in the territory of India or any part thereof, having a distinct language, script or culture of its own shall have the right to conserve the same.

No citizen shall be denied admission into any educational institution maintained by the state or receive aid out of State funds on grounds only of religion, race, caste, language or any of them.[10]

A point that has to be kept in mind while looking at Article 29 is that though it provides protection to the interests of minorities, it does not refer specifically to the minorities whose numerical strength is less. It actually refers to 'any section of the citizens,' who may have a distinct language, script or culture, which means that they may belong even to the majority community. For example, member of the Hindu community living in Punjab or Nagaland will receive protection for their linguistic or cultural rights, by virtue of their being 'so–called minorities' in these States.

A very special fundamental right provided in Article 30 of our Constitution to the religious and linguistic minorities comes next. This is also part of the 'separate domain' provided to the minorities and their members to protect their identity. According to this article:

All minorities, whether based on religion or language shall have the right to establish and administer educational institution of their choice.'

[1A] In making any law pending for the compulsory acquisition of any property of an educational institution established and administered by a minority referred to in clause (1), the State shall ensure that the amount fixed by or determined under such law for the acquisition of such property is such as would not restrict or abrogate the right guaranteed under that clause.]

The State shall not, in granting aid to educational institutions, discriminate against any educational on the ground that it is under the management of a minority, whether based on religion or language.[11]

In brief, these are the basic fundamental or human rights and freedoms, which the Indian Constitution provides in the 'common domain' as well as in the 'separate domain'. In the implementation of these rights and freedoms, of course, care needs to be taken to see that these should be protected in such a way that protection of the minority rights should not take place at the cost of the majority. Asbjorn Eide advice in this regard is worth considering, he says: 'A human rights based quest for minority protection must ... be threefold to search for approach which can safeguard equally between all human beings in society; to promote group diversity where required to ensure the dignity and identity of all and to advance stability and peace, both domestically and internationally[12]. 'With this observation of Eide on the protection of minority rights, I shall now outline the 'role and function of the National

Commission for Minorities in the protection of the human rights of minorities'.

The centre rebutted certain arguments of the Attorney General Soli Sorabhjee, before a 11 judge of the Supreme Court relating to preference being given to minorities under Article 29(2) of the Constitution on July 30, 2002.

Spelling out the Centre's stand, the Solicitor General Harish Salve, submitted before the Bench headed by the Chief Justice, B.N. Kirpal, that "giving of preference by way of extra marks etc., may not be permissible under Article 29(2)."

He said, "it is important to bear in mind that Article 29(2) applies to educational institutions maintained by the State as well as those receiving aid out of the State and treats them on par."

The Solicitor General's submission came pursuant to a letter written by the Human Resource Development Minister, Murli Manohar Joshi, asking him to rebut certain arguments of the AG, who said that by giving preference by way of certain percentage of marks as weightage would be permissible and not hit by Article 29(2).

To a question from the Bench whether an 'added' Minority Educational Institution (MEI) could give weightage to its community, the AG had said that it would be permissible and not hit by Article 29(2), if such a preference was rational and not disproportionate. He maintained that what was rational, whether it was disproportionate or not, would depend on the facts and circumstances prevailing in a particular MEI.

Replying to this, Mr. Salve submitted that if preference were given to minority students in an aided MEI it would create an anomalous situation, as "anything which would be permissible in aided institutions would, therefore, necessarily be permissible in State maintained institution".

He was of the view that "giving additional marks to students only because he belongs to a particular religion would be violation of Article 29(2)".

Referring to the AG's submission that giving preference was based on the promise that there was a positive obligation of the State to fund minority institutions; Mr. Salve said, "there is not such positive obligation contained in the Constitution."

The AG citing various international laws and treaties had asserted before the Bench that under the Constitution minorities were not shown any privilege or concession but they were entitled to their rights.

Mr. Salve, however, said that the analogy given by the AG from international treaties "Is not really appropriate." He said, "international treaties which operate beyond constitutions are quite different from secular democratic constitution which have delicate checks and balances".

He said certain professors and academics had advocated public funding of minority institutions in Europe and positive steps by the State for this purpose. However, the European community had accepted no such principle.

"In fact the 1995 Framework Convention for the Promotion of National Minorities provides to the contrary as it makes right to education subject to regulations made by the State in the field of education", he added. He will continue his arguments tomorrow.

Genesis of Reservation Policy

Primarily, reservation is meant for correcting historical injustice to bring out equality among all, unprivileged brought at par with his fortunate fellow breathen. But the latest placebo statement of U.P. Chief Minister Mr. Rajnath Singh for creating reservation for Most Backward Classes (MBCs) within reservation was merely a political gimmick with an eye on the just concluded Assembly Election in the state. Reservation Policy should not be used as a political weapon nor for creating political constituencies and "vote banks" on the basis of parochial tendencies, ideological affiliations and religious polarization. Therefore, the policy of reservation requires urgent restructuring so that the downtrodden get assimilated in the national life. The policy should not be dispensed with rather be made judicious, plansible and pragmatic.

India has been described as the land of the most inviolable organization by birth. The majority of Indians as much as 85% are Hindus. Since ages past, the nation of caste has been playing very important role in Hindu society. It affects the Indian Society in all aspects of life. India has a unique social system called the caste system, a phenomenon unparalleled in human history. This supposed to be functioning in one form or the other for several thousands years and perhaps is the world's most durable social institution.[13]

In India caste system has its roots in Varna system, a product of wise man's clever thoughts of the time. The earliest description of caste system was found in *Rigveda*, where three groups of people are mentioned: (1) Brahmin, the priest, (2) Kshatriya, the ruler king and (3) Vaishya, the common people. It is also stated that the early society was divided in social classes of varnas on the basis of duties or work but not on the basis of birth. It was only duties performed by a person by which his rank was to be determined.[2]

The post-vedic period experienced the growth and consolidation of the power of the Brahmins. Brahmin writers continued their attempts to define and codify the duties and rights of each caste and its place in the hierarchy. During 18th century some social reform movements i.e. Arya Samaj, Brahmo Samaj, Ramakrishna Mission etc. represented a shift towards the liberalization of caste.

With the advent of the British as the political head of society things were bound to take on a different aspect. The British brought with them their own traditional form of government, and as Christians they could not have much sympathy with the institutions of the Hindus. As prudent foreigners wishing to consolidate their power over a strong land and people they decided to leave the peculiar institutions of the country severely alone except where they egregiously violated their cherished ideas of government. They introduced a system of education which did not demand of the learners any change of religion. Ideas and behaviour patterns, very different from those to which the people were accustomed thus presented as isolated from religion. The policy of comparative non-interference naturally gave scope for the revolt of the castes that were not quite comfortable under the Brahmin supremacy. Later on, with the incoming of the modern industrial organization and the growth of industrial cities, large number of people congregated in cities of mixed populations, away from the influence of their homes and unobserved by their caste or village people.[13]

Consequently, having attained Independence in 1947, some Constitutional measures were initiated and engrafted in the fabric of the Constitution of independent India. The Constitution was not framed for Hindus only. Provision was made for a society heterogeneous in character but secular in outlook. It was a comparative formula, a positive effort to equalize one and all. Even among Hindus where caste system is an institution most highly developed the society is divided into large number of separate groups mostly functional or tribal in origin. By the 20th Century the lowest classes of Hindu society came to be identified as depressed class or untouchables... a name of comparatively recent origin. Rigidly developed over years was partly due to Hindu orthodoxy and partly due to British exploitation.

When the Constitution was framed, the framers were aware of the preferential treatment on religion, race and caste basis. Dr. B.R. Ambedkar while defending the use of the word 'backward' in Drafting Committee explained that "it was to enable other communities to share the services which for historical reasons has been controlled by one community or a few communities. The word community has been defined in *Webster's Comprehensive* Dictionary as, "The people who reside in one locality and are subject to the law, have the same interests, the public as society at large. Further according to *Oxford Dictionary* it means, the quality of appertaining to all in common, ownership, common character. The class was, thus, used in a wider sense and not in the restricted sense of castes.[14]

Historically, therefore, what stated as social upliftment measure for the down-trodden amongst Hindus in some princely states gradually developed into formation of various associations in different states gradually developed into formation of various associations in different states encouraged by the social caste consciousness created by the British to demonstrate backwardness for claiming preferential treatment injected in the society by communal representation.

The thought of a new social order promised on liberty, equality, fraternity and justice to all was at the backbone of the constitution making. The explosive pervasiveness of appalling economic privations and social suppression made this keynote thought the most profound ideology of the Constitution. That is why running right through the wrap and roof of the country's fundamental law, we find a great concern for the weaker sections of the community[15].

Constitutionalisation of Reservation

All human beings born equal and concept of equality[16] was sanctified by every regime, mechanism, order and arrangement ordained by the collective human wisdom as well as by the divine decta. In order to make the right to equality viable, meaningful and pragmatic. Founding Fathers of the Constitution of India have engrafted number of provisions[17] to ameliorate the socio-economic conditions of Backward Class besides the Scheduled Castes and the Scheduled Tribes so as to bring to a level comparable with the advanced sections of our society. The framers of the Constitution were well-acquainted regarding the miserable and pathetic living conditions of this section, which has remained segregated from national and social currents and has been economically oppressed for centuries. Consequently, they resolved in the Preamble to secure to all citizens — social, economic and political and equality of status and opportunity and to promote among them fraternity while assuring the dignity of the individual with the integrity of the nation.

Equality of status and of opportunity... the rubric chiseled in the Preamble of our vibrating and pulsating

Constitution radiates one of the avowed objections in our Sovereign Socialist and Secular Democratic Republic. In every free country, which has adopted a system of government though, democratic principles the people have their fundamental inalienable rights and enjoy the recognition of inherent dignity and of equality analogous to the rights proclaimed in the "Bill of Rights in U.S.A, the 'Rights of Man'" in the French Constitution of 1971 and Declaration of Human Rights etc. Our Constitution is unquestionably unique in its character and assimilation having its notable aspirations contained in Fundamental Right (Part III) through which the illumination of Constitutional rights comes to us not through an artless window glass but refracted with the enhanced intensity and beauty by prismatic interpretation of the Constitutional provisions dealing with equal distribution of justice in the social, political and economic spheres.[18]

The Founding Fathers of our Constitution have designedly and deliberately couched Article 14, 15 and 16 in comprehensive phraseology so that the frail and emaciated section of the people living in poverty, rearing in obscurity, possessing no weather or influence, having no education, much less higher education and suffering from social repression and oppression should not be denied equality before the law or equal protection of the laws: equal opportunity in the matter of public employment or being subjected to any prohibition or discrimination on grounds of religion, race, caste, sex or place of birth etc. For the realization of the above objectives the government enacted innumerable social welfare legislations and geared up social reformative measures for uplifting the social and economic developments of the disadvantaged sections of the people.

Throughout the fifty years life span of the Constitution

of India punctuated with multidimensional schemes, social-justice oriented legislations and commendable judicial pronouncements the question that lurks in all the nooks and corners of our national body politics is whether the principle of equality of status and or, opportunity to be equality provided to all the citizens of the country from cradle to grave is satisfactorily consummated and whether the claims of equality of opportunity in matters of public employment enshrined in Article 16(4) of the Constitution of India has been called into action. The ultimate goal of the constitution of India is to bring about a casteless and classless equalitarian society doing away with the inequalities and inequities inherent in the socio-economic system prevailing in his country.[19]

No class of citizens can be classified as backward solely by reason of religion, race, caste, sex, descent or place of birth, residence or any of them. But any one or all of these factors mentioned in Article 15(1) or Article 16(2) can be taken into account along with other relevant factors in identifying classes of citizens who are socially and educationally backward. What is significant is that such identification should not be made solely with reference to the criteria specified in Article 15(1) or Article 16(2), but with reference to the social and educational backwardness of classes of citizens. Article 15(4), 16(4) and 340(1) do not speak of caste but only of class. Therefore, Muslims also constitute a class and they should also be brought within the protective net of the constitutional scheme.

Historically backwardness has been most acute at the lowest levels of our society and it has been invariably identified with low castes and demeaning occupations but 53 years of independence have charged the social educational and economic landscape beyond recognition. There are crores of backward individuals in forward castes and crores of forward individuals in backward classes[20]. Same is the case with Muslims as they are also sailing the boat of misery and backwardness in every walk of life.

The Supreme Court of India has handed down a series of landmark judgments in relation to social justice by interpreting the constitutional provisions upholding the cherished values of the constitution and thereby had often shaped the course of the national stream of social and economic justice. Notwithstanding a catena of expository decisions with interpretative semantics the stark truth is that no stretch of high or no ray of hope of attaining the equality of status and of opportunity is visible particularly in the case of Muslims.

After the judgment of Mandal Case, providing 27% reservation in the central services and public sector undertakings to other backward classes (OBCs) as per the recommendations of the Mandal Commission Report has created tension between Meritarian principle and the compensatory principle which is also known as principle of redress. The recent political extension of policy of reservation at central level for the first time to newer groups on the basis of caste has created a lot of social tension. Many caste who have been left out of this protective net have started claiming that they are in no way economically, socially and educationally better than those preferred on the basis of Mandal Commission Report. In the 50 years of Constitutional experience in India in the post independence era, their position has also not improved under the conditions of scarcity.[21]

It is really shocking that the policy of reservation is still being used as a political bait to here the masses but the marked truth is that it has benefited those already benefited and its benefits have not trickled down to the most deserving. The present policy has not been persuaded with any serious intention of improving the conditions of the disadvantaged. It only prepares a vote-bank the list of beneficiaries has been lengthening from one election to another, every political party vies with the other to woo scheduled caste and scheduled tribes.

Pursuing Equality: A Case for Muslim's Reservation

The decision of the BJP government to extend reservation to the Jats has once again raised several ineluctable problems for the Indian polity. The problem does not lie with the concept of preferential treatment which has as a supremely normative concept recognizes that all people have a right to equality. In its most familiar form the principle of equality states that if we distribute a good, for example land, among a constituency of ten people, each of the members should get one of the ten parts that we subdivide. Now it is a basic precept of a just legal system that we should compensate those who are not responsible for what has happened to them[22]. In a parallel fashion, we extend historical compensation in the form of reservation to those groups who are not responsible for the discrimination that is practiced against them. Most democratic societies today realize that their histories have been forged through the institutionalization of structures of dominance and exclusion, and that the victims of history should be compensated for the wrongs that the dominant groups have unleashed on them. Thus, we make the move from formal to substantive equality, from equalitarianism to egalitarianism. And it is this feature of equality that makes it a desirable principle for any society claiming to be an egalitarian democracy[23]. Therefore, we accept the principle of historical compensation on reservation as an integral feature of our polity and social structure.

Since Independence Muslim community is being alienated in such a way where they find themselves helpless and rudderless. The deprivation in any form particularly of the largest minority of the Indian nation would never be in the larger interest of the country alienation of any section of the people of India will lead to morass, anarchy, and chaos in the country. Even after the 50 years of Independence and constitutional guarantees, the Muslims trail behind from others in educational, status, income and employment in public and private sectors in politics. In all this sound and fury we must tend to extend reservation to Muslim who are today multiply disadvantaged. The position of the Muslims at the lowest rung of the social hierarchy and their corresponding lack of economic status is the compelling reason to improve their position through reservation.

Therefore, the most vexed and pertinent problem relating to reservation is *reservation for religious minorities.* The experiences of the last fifty years indicate differential and uneven development, wherein some sections of society have made rapid advancement and the others have been lagging far behind.

This differential development is more applicable in the case of Muslims. Majority of the Muslims are subjected to relative deprivation. Their educational backwardness is now an established fact. Their representation in government jobs is least visible. Their presence in the legislative and local bodies is meager. These facts have been highlighted in different empirical studies. Though the governmental data are not available to the scholars working on these areas. The NGOs and concerned individuals have been collecting data on these aspects. These reveal the relative backwardness of the Muslims among all the religious groups. Therefore, there is high time to pay attention to the backwardness of a major section of our population. In the name of unity and integrity of the nation and especially due to the phobia of the harried and horrified experiences of partition of India, reservations to the Muslims have interpreted as counter-productive. Any effective and important measure exclusively for the uplift of the Muslims has not been taken. The step taken by the government for the welfare of the minorities does not appear sufficient. Therefore, some effective form of *affirmative action is required for the needs of the Muslim community.* The exact criteria could be evolved in this regard, which would guide the policy. Secondly, there is no denying the fact that the Muslims are not adequately represented in the government services. *The provision of Article 16(4) may be extended to the Muslims with the provisions of creamy layer and Annexure system.* A detailed modality can be worked out with team of experts. It needs to be reiterated that their exclusion from the structure of governance may lead to a great extent of alienation, which, in turn would be contradictory to the constitutional spirit, and vision of the founding fathers.

Agenda Ahead

The center rebutted certain arguments of the Attorney General Soli Sorabjee, before an 11 judge of the Supreme Court relating to preference being given to minorities under Article 29(2) of the Constitution on July 30, 2002.

Spelling out the center's stand, the Solicitor General Harish Salve, submitted before the Bench headed by the Chief Justice, B.N. Kirpal, that "giving of preference by way of extra marks etc. may not be permissible under Article 29(2)."

He said, "it is important to bear in mind that Article

29(2) applies to educational institutions maintained by the State as well as those receiving aid out of the State and treats them on par."

The Solicitor General's submission came pursuant to a letter written by the Human Resource Development Minister, Murli Manohar Joshi, asking him to rebut certain arguments of the AG, who said that by giving preference by way of certain percentage of marks as weightage would be permissible and not hit by Article 29(2).

To a question from the Bench whether an 'added' Minority Educational Institution (MEI) could give weightage to its community, the AG had said that it would be permissible and not hit by Article 29(2), if such a preference was rational and not disproportionate. He maintained that what was rational, whether it was disproportionate or not, would depend on the facts and circumstances prevailing in a particular MEI.

Replying to this, Mr. Salve submitted that if preference were given to minority students in an aided MEI it would create an anomalous situation, as "anything which would be permissible in aided institutions would, therefore, necessarily be permissible in State maintained institution".

He was of the view that "giving additional marks to students only because he belongs to a particular religion would be violation of Article 29(2)".

Referring to the AG's submission that giving preference was based on the promise that there was a positive obligation of the State to fund minority institutions; Mr. Salve said, "there is not such positive obligation contained in the Constitution".

The AG citing various international laws and treaties had asserted before the Bench that under the Constitution minorities were not shown any privilege or concession but they were entitled to their rights.

Mr. Salve, however, said that the analogy given by the AG from international treaties "Is not really appropriate." He said, "international treaties which operate beyond constitutions are quite different from secular democratic constitution which have delicate checks and balances."

He said certain professors and academics had advocated public funding of minority institutions in Europe and positive steps by the State for this purpose. However, the European community had accepted no such principle.

"In fact the 1995 Framework Convention for the Promotion of National Minorities provides to the contrary as it makes right to education subject to regulations made by the State in the field of education," he added.

Earlier, on behalf of Karnataka it was submitted that the court should lay guidelines to ensure that unscrupulous or unprincipled individuals of bodies did not hijack constitution provisions for subserving ulterior purposes and establish an institution in the guise of the MEI.

The State was of the view that though MEI had the right to regulate admission of its student's reasonable restrictions could be imposed conducive to the welfare of the institution. Also minority rights could not be used as a cloak for promotion of individual or family interests.

It is submitted that maintaining standards of education were not a part of management as such. MEIs could not be allowed to fall below the standards of excellence expected of educational institutions or under the guise of exclusive rights of management to decline to follow the general pattern.

Further, MEIs must go by a self-imposed set of regulations that would ensure the most meritorious amongst the minorities alone would be selected and that the means of selection would not be converted to conferring undeserved benefits upon their favorites and inferior students for reasons unconnected with academic excellence.

Conclusion

The undignified social status and sub-human living conditions of Muslims leave an indelible impression that their forlorn hopes for equality in every sphere of life are only a myth rather a reality. It is verily believed, rightly too, that the one and only peerless way and indeed a most important and promising way to achieve the equal status and equal opportunity is only by means of constitutional justice so that all the citizens of this country irrespective of the religion, race, caste, sex, place of birth or any of them may achieve the goal of an egalitarian society.

Any package of reservation must aim at removing the socio-legal disabilities of the Muslims to facilitate their equal participation in the national mainstream and to protect them against social injustice and exploitation. The entire mechanism of protective discrimination has been designed by the Founding Fathers of our Constitution to be used as an engine of social and economic restructuring and engineering. Reservations are meant not only for correcting historical injustice but also existing injustice must also be corrected by the reservation. The basic postulate should be that Muslim must also be brought at par with their fortunate fellow brethren.

Thus, the reservation policy requires urgent restructuring so that the Muslims get integrated in the national mainstream. What is required and imperative, therefore, is not to scrap the policy but to make it judicious, sagacious and pragmatic. The major thrust at the moment should be to help the Muslims while extending to them the protective net of reservation as envisioned under the Constitution of India for SCs, STs and OBCs and we should ponder over the whole scheme with new thrusts and alterations.

NOTES & REFERENCES

1. Media Development, No. 4/1988, Vol. XXXV, *Journal of the World Association for Christian Communication*, London, p. 1.
2. *Manual on Human Rights Reporting*, under six major International Human Rights Instruments, United Nations, Geneva, 1997, pp. 4-5.
3. Dr. Patrick Thornberry, *Minorities and Human Rights Law*, A Minority Rights Group Report, London, 1991, p. 11.
4. Iqbal A. Ansari (ed.) *Readings on Minorities Perspectives and Documents*, Vol. 1. New Delhi, 1996, p. 220.
5. *Ibid.*, p. 311.
6. *Manual on Human Rights Reporting*, op. cit., pp. 6-7.
7. Iqbal A. Ansari (ed.), *Readings on Minorities: Perspectives and Documents*, Vol. 2, New Delhi, 1996, pp. 508, 512-13.
8. Asbjorn Eide, *New Approaches to Minority Protection*, Minority Right Group, London, 1991, p. 12.
9. The Constitution of India (as on 1 June 1996), Government of India, New Delhi 1996, prelims.
10. *Ibid., op. cit.*, p. 15.
11. *Ibid., op. cit.*, pp. 5-9.
12. *Ibid.*, p. 9.
13. Ishwari Prasad, *Reservation Action For Social Equality*, p. 39 (1986).
14. Marya S.D. Gayatri Devi, *Social Environment of India Caste System*. 1989, p. 105.

15. G.S. Ghurye, *Caste And Races in India* (1969) p. 27.
16. *Indira Sahney v. Union of India* (1939) SCJ, p. 542.
17. V.R. Krishna Iyer, *Social Engineering and Constitutional Protection of Weaker Sections in India* (Foreword) by Anirudh Prasad, 1986.
18. Article 14, The Constitution of India.
19. Article 15, 16.
20. Supra note 4. Justice Pandian, p. 372.
21. D.S. Prakash Rao, "The Implementation of Mandal Commission Report: An Unequal Distribution of Benefit, *S.C.J.* 1992 Vol. 1, p. 39.
22. N.A. Palkiwala, "Mandal Perpetuates Casteism." *The Hindu*, Nov. 11, 1992, New Delhi Edition.
23. Supra note 1, p. 30.
24. Neera Chandhoke, "Rethinking Reservation," *The Hindu*, Nov. 4, 1999, New Delhi Edition.
25. *Ibid.*

3

INDIAN MUSLIMS: THEIR ROLE, PROBLEMS AND PROSPECTS

— *Kumkum Kishore*

"A group of people differentiated by others in the same society by race, nationality, religion and language" is how contemporary sociologists generally define the term minority—a group relatively lacking in power and as a result subjected to certain discrimination and differential treatment.

It is documented that in India the various communities have lived together for centuries with a bond of unity of culture and tradition—a unification which despite differences and conflicts often inspired this nation in the event of a national crisis and threat of war.

With the adoption of the Constitution of India, *equality* became the watchword. Within India—a nation that has arisen to become a modern democracy with equal rights and opportunities, freedom and liberty to all citizens, there are still minority communities which harbour feelings of *separateness*. Even when there are no physical differences in the people of these communities, yet, prejudices are ingrained and are enduring.

Three major issue areas relevant for all Muslim minorities can be visualised, namely,

- *Poverty*
- *Threat* from 'majority' which may be perceived as a threat to their *identity* (India and China), and,
- The *role* of Muslim minority amongst the larger society of which they are a part.

Poverty today may also mean *illiteracy*. Society in the 21st century is definitely becoming more competitive. In the world of tomorrow, nothing will move without education and economic strength, and in India a country encompassing within itself a variety of ethnic, linguistic and religious groups, this implies that every group, every community will have to *mobilise its own resources* to preserve its identity and promote its culture.

The poor are free only in name. They cannot be expected to actively participate in the meaningful contribution to civil society and gradually it is seen that they tend to develop a grudge towards the society which can lead to other related problems. So the questions which prey upon the mind are: What prevents Muslims from playing the desired role in society? and, how far are the Muslims themselves responsible for their seemingly 'disadvantaged' state?

Constituting more than 12% of the Indian population it stands to reason that the economic and educational progress of the Muslims be ensured by the Government and the problems which can broadly be termed as socio-economic (widespread illiteracy, low income, irregular employment and high incidence of poverty pointing to a low level of human development) must be dealt with adequately. (The report of the subgroup on Minorities, 1996, constituted by the Planning Commission illustrates that there are no signs of any significant improvement).

Educational backwardness reflects economic backwardness and scarcity of economic resources can perpetrate educational backwardness, hence economic betterment and raising educational levels are necessary conditions, if any meaningful role is to be played by Muslim minority *vis-à-vis* its countrymen. In fact it is a precondition for survival. Banks and financial institutions can play an important role and here one would like to mention that the *Wakf properties* in India are capable of generating massive internal resources for the benefit of the Muslim community.

The National Policy on Education has emphasised on greater attention to educate the educationally backward minority groups and a number of schemes have been envisaged for their development which have been undertaken by the central and state governments.

A view which comes to mind and which has also been lent support to by some political activists is the establishing of *common schools* for children — schools for modern secular education (of both majority and minority groups having uniform pattern of teaching and syllabi) where they would get the opportunity to *integrate in a heterogeneous environment.*

Reference may at this juncture be made to two (of six) crises which are faced by any society or nation in the process of its development – crisis of identity (the sense of oneness and belonging with the nation) and crisis of penetration (of Government policies and programmes percolating to the grass-roots and the target group).

The Indian Constitution recognises plural identities in its society and within this plural polity, it is till possible to have both equality and identity, the development of which has to be based on national integration of the tenets of social justice, political democracy and economic progress.

Quoting verbatim from an article by Akhtar Majeed entitled "Minorities and Nation-State" would be apt this juncture: "the role of the minority elite and of the so-called minority leadership is no less in perpetuating the deplorable socio-economic and political conditions of their community. Since the minority elite is a minority within a minority, it can maintain its privileges only through mechanisms of patronage and safeguards from the majority. Through co-option by the majority, which provides patronage to pliable yet vocal sections of minorities, it is possible for the minority elite to appropriate to themselves the meagre political-economic opportunities that, theoretically, might have been available to the community. What is blatantly ridiculous is the fact that while such an elite obtains whatever benefits are available because it is a minority-elite, they over-react to this situation by trying to de-emphasise the fact that they belong to a minority. Further, the issues that are raised by such an elite has nothing to do with the real down-to-earth problems of the community but they are the issues that unite people as a community, thus ensuring the leadership of the elite. It is also a fact that the moment such an elite tries to raise the real socio-economic problems faced by the minorities, they are termed as fanatic, fundamentalist, communal, and even anti-national. They, therefore, easily learn the lesson that, by mixing religion with politics in airing their demands, they have a better chance of being taken seriously and in this, they are assisted by the government also which looks seriously only in those grievances which center around religion. The insecurities arising out of perceived deprivation can be played upon by political rabble-rousers and dream-merchants, from the ranks of the minority leadership and the national leadership, both."

Indira Gandhi had emphasised her commitment to

the secular ideal. It would be apt at this juncture to repeat her statement, made way back in 1983 when she had stated, "the India of our dreams, can survive only if Muslims and other minorities can live in absolute safety and confidence."

Any government worth its name, that seeks to empower the minorities in its attempt towards development and socio-economic progress must genuinely focus upon its *backward and forward linkages* and must therefore:

- — review the existing approaches and strategies;
- — identify those areas for minority upliftment requiring immediate attention;
- — devise mechanisms leading to effective implementation of government schemes;
- — make efforts for redressal of inequities and imbalances;
- — resolve the identity crisis which can prove to be a major hurdle in the cause for common bonding;
- — Foster a positive political will to implement safeguards for protection of the rights of minorities.

The *role* of Muslim minority has to be *participatory*, and if there is an *isolationist attitude* it needs to be shed for their own benefit. Their *socio-political leadership* must reflect more *vision*. Resort to an 'ism', to an ideology without rationalising it, may also be a significant factor for their disadvantaged position.

Prospects depend on the role and problems. If their (Muslims) role is more favourable and the problems are viewed more dispassionately and dealt in a more enlightened and sustainable basis, the prospects would be that much better.

After all they form a continuum.

REFERENCES

1. Majeed Akhtar (Ed.), *Nation and Minorities: India's Plural Society and its Constituent*, Kanishka Publications, Distributors, New Delhi.
2. Hasan, M., *Legacy of a Divided Nation—India's Muslims since Independence.*
3. *The Eastern Anthropologist*, Volume 53, No. 3-4, July-December 2000.

PART – II

SOCIO-ECONOMIC STATUS

4

SOCIO-ECONOMIC DEVELOPMENT OF MUSLIMS IN URBAN SETTLEMENTS OF AVADH REGION, UTTAR PRADESH: A COMPARATIVE ANALYSIS

— *S.S.A. Jafri*

Muslims being the second largest religious majority community of the world and in India as a whole, is rarely undertaken by the social scientists to analyse their levels of socio-economic development in comparison to its counterpart majority community. It is most important to highlight the reasons of their comparative backwardness, especially after Independence and its consequences leading to underdevelopment in India and the world as a whole. It is obvious that if all the communities are not equally developed, no region, no country and even world can develop. Social scientists have already established the fact that the social conflicts are always due to unequal opportunities among the communities, which further erode the overall development.

In this study, the urban primary data from random sample survey (collected by the author and his team for the Institute's SUDA project*) has been analysed to see the levels of socio-economic development among Muslims in comparison to total as well as forward (Hindu and Muslim population combined) in Avadh region. All the towns and cities were surveyed in six districts namely Lucknow, Rae Bareli, Unnao, Hardoi, Sitapur and Lakhimpur Kheri. Among six cities (which are also district Headquarters) and 61 small and medium towns, total 1581 random households were surveyed. In which 29.03 per cent or 459 households belonged to Muslims, 36.30 per cent or 574 households (Hindu 25.11 and Muslims 11.9 per cent households) belonged to forward community.

Population Structure

Overall Muslim male children of 0-14 years age group are 29.6 per cent, which are 2.5 per cent more than the male children of forward community, but 1.4 per cent lower than the total male children. Here explanation can also be given that majority of Muslims are economically and socially poor (majority of people belong to lowest caste), as at least 61.454 per cent Muslims are reported to be Backward as per government recognition. Sociologically, lower caste denotes that overall economically and socially deprived, which means higher birth rates. Even then, here Muslim male children are found proportionately lower than the total average. It means that the practice of family planning among Muslims is more than the overall population in average, but of course less than the forward community.

Proportion of female children of age group 0-14 years is higher by 1.06 and 7.26 per cent among the Muslim female population in comparison to proportion among

---

* SSA Jafri, "Evaluation of Swarna Jayanti Shahri Rozgar Yojana (SJSRY) and National Slums Development Programme (NSDP), 1999-2000 in Lucknow Division of Uttar Pradesh", sponsored by SUDA, 2001.

total females and females of forward community respectively. The explanation of Muslim female population having more proportion of female children, can be given that in most part of India due to dowry, females are considered social and economic burden among the majority population in general and among it's forward castes in particular. Therefore, it is already a reality that among the majority in general and its forward caste in particular the practice of female discrimination to female elimination (infanticide) is quite common. In recent censuses of 1981,1991 and 2002 the reducing trend of sex ratio among 0-6 years age group, females per 1000 males 962,945 and 927 respectively, which were quite serious and it shook the entire nation.* Proportionately Muslim female children are comparatively less in comparison to total female children in only Lucknow and Unnao districts. Similarly, as exception in Lakhimpur proportion of female children is less than the female children among the forward community.

In children of age group 0-14 years, the sex ratio, i.e. females per 1000 males among Muslims is higher with 1333 than the total 1239 and forward community only 1186. Except in Unnao district where sex ratio among Muslim children is less than the total children as well as the children of forward population. In all other districts the sex ratio among Muslim children is higher than the children of forward population, with again the exception in Lakhimpur district, where the sex ratio among the children of forward population is higher. This sex ratio also supports

---

* Anudhuti Roy Chaudhary, "Death of the Unborn Girl", *Hindustan Times*, Lucknow, October 25, 2002, p. 6.

In Punjab, sex ratio is 793, Haryana 820 and Delhi 845. *Saheli* a Delhi based women's group estimates that during 1978-82 in Delhi about 76000 female fetuses were aborted. During 1987-88 in Delhi 13000 sex determination tests were done in only 7 clinics.

the hypothesis of female discrimination to female elimination (female infanticides) as ongoing phenomenon among total children in general and among children of forward community in particular. Though Islam strictly prohibits the abortion and considers it a serious crime equivalent to committing a murder. It is feared that if this evil practice of female infanticide is not strictly prohibited, then the other communities may not stay without getting infected, like social abuse of dowry demand in marriages, which has clearly taken the society into its clutches.

Working age group (15-59 years) is the backbone of the society for its livelihood. In Lucknow division overall among male population 67.60 per cent are working age people, when among forward and Muslim communities this proportion is 67.63 per cent and 67.09 per cent respectively, which are almost equal. Among Muslims males the proportion of working age group is higher than the proportion of total and forward population in towns/ cities of Lucknow, Rae Bareli, Hardoi and Lakhimpur districts. As an exception in Unnao and Sitapur districts males of forward working age population are higher than the Muslim males.

Among Muslim females, the proportion of working age population is 56.75 per cent, which is lower than the proportions in total 58.50 per cent and forward 62.18 per cent female population. Forward working age group females are proportionately quite high than the proportion of total and Muslim working age group females. This may be because of higher female proportion in employment among the forward community in urban areas. The higher proportion of female working age group of forward community are in Lucknow 65.25, Rae Bareli 65.46, Hardoi 70.43 and Sitapur 60.34, while in Lakhimpur it is 47.50 per cent, which is contrary, i.e. less than 62.18 per cent of total female working age group.

Overall sex ratio among working age population shows that forward community has sex ratio, which is above the average, i.e. 919, while Muslims are quite below the average with 846 sex ratio. In Lucknow, Hardoi and Sitapur districts sex ratio among forward community is quite high than the average, i.e. 927, 977 and 903 respectively. Only in Rae Bareli the sex ratio is above 1000 among total population 1130 and forward castes 1081, which is highest in working age group.

Old age groups of 60 years and above in total male and female surveyed population is only 4.0 and 3.1 per cent respectively. Among forward community the old age male and female proportion is highest, i.e. 5.34 and 4.12 per cent respectively, when old age Muslim males are only 3.39 and females are only 2.99 per cent, which are lowest and below the average. Except in Hardoi and Lakhimpur districts, the proportions of forward old age males are quite high in all the other districts than the average. Similarly, except Sitapur district, proportions of forward females are higher than average in all the other districts. Old age Muslim males and females are proportionately below the average and all the districts except in Hardoi and Lakhimpur districts. Overall sex ratios among total, forward and Muslims are below 1000, and comparatively quite high in Muslims with 882 females per 1000 males. It indicates that Muslim old age females have better survival trend than the average as well as forward people of old age group. In Lucknow, Hardoi and Sitapur districts, sex ratio among old age Muslim is below than the average. Sex ratios of old age Muslims cross 1000 in Rae Bareli 1440 and in Lakhimpur 2023, and in case of total old age population in Sitapur

1120 and in Lakhimpur 1143, when among old age forward community sex ratio is highest with 2604.

Marital status among the Muslim males and females is lowest, i.e. 42.75 and 40.10 per cent in comparison to total and forward community males and females which are 45.30, 43.90 and 44.85, 47.26 per cent respectively, which correlates according to their affordability. Only in Hardoi, Muslim males and females are proportionately more married in comparison to total and forward community males and females. Widowed and divorced proportions of males with 1.70 per cent and females with 2.67 per cent among Muslims is quite matching with the total male and female average, whereas among forward community widowed and divorced are 2.25 and 3.55 per cent respectively, which are quite high. In Hardoi no male and female and in Rae Bareli no male is widowed and divorced.

Educational Level

Overall literacy among Muslim males and females are 69.89 and 55.70 per cent respectively, which is comparatively less than the total and forward community male and female literacy by 6.51, 3.70 and 13.40, 12.47 per cent respectively. Muslims are showing overall comparative backwardness in literacy, besides that Muslim females are comparatively less lagging behind than their counterpart males. In Hardoi district, urban Muslim male and female literacy is quite low in comparison to total male, female by 25.00, 25.75 and to forward male, female by 21.86,32.07 per cent respectively. As an exception in Unnao district Muslim male literacy is higher than both the total and forward males, whereas Muslim female literacy is only higher in comparison to total female, which is of course with insignificant difference. In case of educated (those who have attended schools at any stage) among males and females of total, (forward and Muslims are more or less the same as the proportion of literate.

Proportions of Muslim male and female school pass are less in comparison to total male and female by 0.47, 2.72 and to forward castes male and female by 1.90, 5.86 per cent respectively. In Rae Bareli district proportionately High School pass females are quiet high than their counterpart males, where total, forward castes and Muslim females High School pass are proportionately 6.60, 11.49 and 7.55 per cent respectively higher than their counterpart males to whom it is an eye opener. In Unnao and Sitapur districts, Muslim males are proportionately more High School pass than among total and forward caste male population. In Hardoi district Muslim females are proportionately more High School passes than total and forward caste females.

Proportion of Intermediate pass among Muslim males and females is quite lower than proportion in total urban population by male 4.11, female 2.32 and by forward caste male 7.28, female 4.10 per cent respectively. We can observe that Muslim males and females Intermediate pass have further slided than their proportion, which was in High School pass. In Unnao and Lakhimpur districts it is quite high. In Unnao and Lakhimpur districts, Muslim females are proportionately more intermediate pass than total and forward caste proportions.

The proportion of graduation (BA+) and above pass has slightly further gone down in Muslim male and female population than it was in High School and intermediate pass. If it is compared with total and forward caste proportions it is lower by male 5.10, female 3.86 and male 7.72, female 5.78 per cent respectively. In Unnao district graduate pass overall male and female proportions are too low than other districts. In Hardoi district no Muslim male or female was graduate pass, when Muslims in Rae Bareli both males and females, in Unnao and Lakhimpur districts males and in Sitapur district females were less 2.00 per cent graduates. Only in Unnao district Muslim females were proportionately more graduates than the total and forward caste proportions, which is an exception. Other significant phenomenon is found that except in Hardoi and Sitapur districts in rest of districts like Lucknow, Rae Bareli, Unnao and Lakhimpur, the proportion of Muslim female graduates are higher than their counterpart Muslim males.

Dependent and Employment

It is important to analyze various categories of dependents and their pressure on employed population for overall economic development. In case of precaution of students, which is an indicator of future development as the more educated and qualified population would be there the more overall developed community would be there and vice-versa. The proportions of students in Muslim male and female population is 26.72 and 26.60 per cent respectively, which is less by 1.38 per cent in males and more by 0.30 per cent in females in comparison to total male and female population. Muslim male and female proportions of students are less by male 2.21 and female 0.34 per cent in comparison to proportions of forward male and female students. One very micro observation can be highlighted that the proportion of male and female students in Muslim community is almost balanced, male students are 0.12 per cent higher than female students are when difference in proportion of male and female students of total population is 1.80 and in forward community it is 1.99percent. it means that forward community female are comparatively more discriminated against their counter part males than females belonging to total and Muslim population. In Rae Bareli and Hardoi districts Muslim male and female proportion of students are less by 5 to 10 per cent in comparison to total and forward males and females. The proportion of students among Muslim population is higher in females than their counterpart males in district of Lucknow, Hardoi and Sitapur. In Sitapur and Lakhimpur districts the proportion of both Muslim male and female students are comparatively higher that total and forward males and females. This shows that no community can be backward educationally so long their social and economic environment is congenial (as it already happened that discrimination and step-motherly treatment lead to SC, ST and Backward community's reservation now to be followed by the minorities, who are also demanding for reservation).

Children of 0-14 years age group, in which roughly about 5 per cent infants of less than 3 years age are also included who hardly go to school is a universal phenomenon. The picture emerges that both forward male and female children are in low proportion in comparison to total and Muslim male and female children, who do not go to school, with only one exception among male children in Unnao district.

Non-working old age people (60+) are comparatively more in both the success (male 5.08, female 4.00 per cent) of forward population than the total and Muslim population, which is quite natural as old age people are well cared in well-off families of forward castes. While Muslim non-working old age men are 3.08 per cent, which slightly less than the total males when their females are 3.72 per cent which are proportionately more than the total proportion of females non-working old age.

Overall unemployment in male working age group (15-59 is about 10.0 per cent in total and forward population, both among Muslims is 13.45 per cent, which is a matter of worry. Except Hardoi district, in rest of the other districts this male unemployment proportion is more among Muslims than the total and forward working age group population. Male working age unemployed varies between 40 to 50 per cent among total forward and Muslim working age population. When this proportion of female working age employment is highest in Rae Bareli district which is between 50 to 65 per cent among total, forward and Muslims. Similarly this female unemployment is lowest in proportion in Lakhimpur district for total, forward and Muslims.

Roughly half of the male population is engaged in one or the other economic activities, may be total, forward or Muslims. In case of economically engaged females which are proportionately less than 5.00 per cent in all the three social categories of total, forward and Muslims. Only as an exception in Hardoi district both males and females of Muslims are proportionately more engaged in economic activities than compared to total and forward females. In Unnao district no Muslim female was recorded who could be engaged economically, when among total and forward females, the proportion was 0.30 and 0.47 per cent respectively, which are negligible.

Employment in Various Occupations

Employments as laboureres, which are generally daily wage earners are about 21.94 per cent in males and 12.41 per cent in females of total persons economically employed. Among Muslims labourers are almost more or less the same in proportion like total, as 20.99 per cent males and 10.26 per cent females are labourers. However, among forwards the proportion is almost half than the total as

9.04 per cent males and 5.00 per cent females are labourers. In Sitapur proportion of female labourers are more than double than males in all the social groups of total, forward and Muslims. In Unnao and Hardoi no Muslim females was found engaged as labourer. Similarly, in Rae Bareli, Unnao, Hardoi and Lakhimpur districts no female from forward caste was engaged as labourer.

Artisans or Misteries are comparatively more among Muslims, especially among their females, which are 41.03 per cent, when males are 16.67 per cent, in comparison, Muslim females artisans are more than double of total and forward female population. In Unnao and Lakhimpur districts no female artisans were found. Also as an exception in Sitapur no Muslim female artisan was recorded. In Rae Bareli district Muslim female artisans were comparatively less than the total and forward female population. It is to mention that in Lucknow and its environ chicken work is dominating, which is world famous.

In business Muslim males are slightly above the average but less than the forward caste, whereas proportion caste females that it is about half. In business activity forward castes males and females are proportionately above the average when only males of Muslims are above the average. As usual Unnao district no Muslim woman was recorded in our survey as engaged in any economic activity. Only in Sitapur district Muslim males are proportionately engaged in business than the average and forward castes males. In Unnao and Lakhimpur Districts total and forward caste women are proportionately more engaged in business than their counterpart males.

The most desired occupation is the government job, which assures the guaranteed payment and most comfortable from all angles. That is the reason that in

India whenever any social group which comes into power, socially, politically or economically, grabs the most lucrative government jobs, which are already limited in number and which makes social and economic disparity in other groups. Exactly due to discrimination as already stated government was compelled to reserve seats' for SC, ST and OBC despite extreme opposition. Among minorities in India this disparity is felt since long and the vehement voices are being raised for their job reservation as done for other deprive groups and communities.

Out of total employment in various occupations, in government jobs 6.21 per cent among males and 4.14 per cent among females are engaged in Avadh Region. From this average base when we compare we find that the males and females of forward castes (includes religious majority and minority) are one and a half times, i.e. males 9.04 per cent and double and females 8.33 per cent respectively. But, if Muslims are compared in government jobs, they are roughly one-third among males and nil among females. This is a great anomaly and main reason of turmoil in all walks of life in our great democratic country. Where selfishly connived imposition of apartheid conditions, which exists in pockets. The entire lot of SC, ST, OBC and minorities, which form a majority of India's roughly 1020 million population suffer from partisan attitude of few who are socially and economically powerful. In all the six districts no where any Muslim female was found employed in government job in our survey. In Hardoi district even no Muslim male was found in government job. In Unnao and Sitapur districts only less than 2.0 per cent Muslim males are in government jobs. Only in Lakhimpur district 5.26 per cent Muslim males are in government jobs which is a highest proportion, but their counter part males in total and forward population are 6.51 and 17.65 per cent respectively. Private jobs which are hardly permanent and inept itself sustainment and at the mercy of their master overall females dominate may be total forward or Muslims. Here also Muslims males are quite below the average and below the proportion of forward castes. Among all the economic activities, Muslim females are engaged more than a quarter in private jobs, that is 25.64 per cent. In Unnao and Hardoi districts no Muslims females were recorded in private jobs. Among working Muslims females, the private jobs (mainly domestic servants) where they are in considerable proportion for example in Rae Bareli 50.00, Sitapur 33.33, Lakhimpur 25.00 and Lucknow 23.53 per cent.

Housing Condition

In our random survey of 1581 beneficiaries who were also enquired about their housing condition. Out of which 36.30 per cent houses belonged to Muslims. Among Muslims, they had 89.98 per cent houses as their own, which is more than the ownership among total and forward households and 10.02 per cent were on rent. In Rae Bareli district all the Muslim households owned their houses and no one was in rented house. The lowest ownership of houses among Muslims was 74.07 per cent in Hardoi district, due to which 25.93 per cent households lived in rented houses, which is highest. On asking whether you have constructed your own house on your own land, or on encroached land? Overall 0.22 per cent Muslims constructed their houses on other's land (encroached land), when among total houses, about 0.80 per cent houses on encroached land. In Lucknow district about 0.62 per cent houses belonging to Muslims are on encroached lands, when among total houses 0.90 per cent houses were found on encroached lands.

For quality of housing, they were categorized under pucca, semi-pucca and kutcha. Overall among total houses pucca were 67.00, semi-pucca 22.40 and kutcha 10.60 per cent, when houses belonging to Muslims were pucca 65.14, semi pucca 22.00 and kutcha 12.86 per cent. And if compared to houses belonging to forward castes, they were pucca 82.42, semi pucca 16.12 and kutcha 3.47 per cent.

Muslims have lowest average number of rooms in their houses, i.e., 2.14, when average 2.30 rooms are in overall houses and 2.50 rooms in forward castes houses Muslims families having less than the average number of rooms in their houses are found in districts of Lucknow, Rae Bareli, Unnao and Hardoi with 2.13, 2.10, 1.89 and 2.59 rooms per house hold / house respectively. Overall housing situation in rural as well as in urban areas is not quite well as compared to developed and even developing countries. In India (rural and urban about 40 per cent households huddle in one room set of house, which is as good as living direct under sky, because that room works only as a store of the family.

Overall Muslim occupied houses are comparatively more electrified, that is 82.14 per cent than the overall total houses, which are 82.00 per cent, but Muslims occupied houses are about 10.06 per cent less electrified than the houses belonging to forward castes which are 92.20 per cent. In Lakhimpur district Muslim occupied houses are 64.29 per cent electrified which is lowest, when entire forward castes houses are electrified.

Muslims occupied houses in urban areas of Awadh region have 76.25 per cent houses with latrines within the campus, which is more than the total houses with 68.50 per cent latrines within the campus. However, forward castes have about 84.58 per cent of their residences with latrines. In all the districts except Hardoi, were in average Muslims occupied houses are proportionately more with latrines within their campuses. The most worrying things are that in Rae Bareli district total average houses are 43.30 latrines within the campus, when Muslim occupied houses are 52.94 per cent with latrines, and forward castes with 63.46 per cent latrines, within the campus, which is lowest. Overall Muslim occupied houses having latrines within the campus are comparatively less with flush, i,e, 54.28 per cent and dry 45.72 per cent which are more. When total average houses are 58.10 per cent with flush and 41.90 per cent are dry compared to houses occupied by forward castes are 56.15 per cent flush and 43.80 per cent dry. Overall situation in Hardoi, Sitapur and Lakhimpur districts is worst, where house of total, forward and Muslims are having maximum proportion of dry latrines, ranging between 40 to 80 percent. In Lucknow, Rae Bareli and Unnao districts about 10 to 40 per cent house of total, forward castes and Muslims are having dry latrines. One can imagine that every day head loads of night soil is disposed off through the urban streets, creating a filthy and obnoxious environment in urban life. It is already an urban curse that about 20 to 30 per cent households defecate on the street as they do not have latrines within their campus, as public latrines are generally negligible or not usable.

Muslim occupied houses, which have bathrooms, are 69.50 per cent, when total houses and houses occupied by forward castes are with 67.60 per cent and 77.30 per cent bathrooms within premises respectively. In Unnao district the houses with bathrooms within the campus are least, as total houses with bathrooms are 35.80 per cent, houses occupied by forward castes and Muslims with 38.46 and 43.06 per cent respectively. In absence of bathrooms within the house campus, people take bath at the public places generally where public water taps or handpumps are located and create an absence in urban life. For ladies it is further difficult in absence of any privacy.

Availability of source of drinking water (water taps or handpumps) within the residential campus is an important aspect of busy urban life. Overall 66.20 per cent houses have their own water sources within the campus, when forward caste occupied houses have 78.86 per cent and Muslim occupied houses have 67.32 per cent with water source. It means that 33.80 per cent of total households, 21.14 per cent of forward caste households and 32.68 per cent of Muslim households depend on outside water source, which is an alarming proportion. In Rae Bareli district situation is worst, where 52.10 per cent total, 4.38 per cent forward caste and 50.98 per cent Muslim households have to fetch water from outside sources. Even in Lucknow district where households of total population forward castes and Muslims, which are 36.2, 21.68 and 35.62 per cent respectively have to fetch water from outside sources.

Houses, which are flooded with rain or drain water, impose a bad taste in urban life from health and hygiene point of view. Overall 44.10 per cent houses are either affected by rain or drain flood almost throughout the year, when forward castes and Muslims occupied houses are affected by 32.06 and 39.21 per cent respectively. In Lakhimpur, Lucknow and Hardoi districts the proportion of flood affected houses are maximum among total, 58.80, 55.60, 47.80; among forward castes 39.53, 36.28, 52.19; and Muslims 48.57, 50.63, 44.45 per cent respectively. These are the defects of urban planning in which drainage system are not seriously considered in Masterplans that even well established colonies of LDA/Awas-Vikas in state capital of Lucknow are affected by rain or drain flood.

Conclusion

It is a wrong notion that Muslim population growth is faster than the average population growth rate. In this study proportion of average Muslim male children of 0-14 years (which concerns more in growth rate of population is 1:4 per cent lower than the male children of average total population. The proportion of Muslim female children of 0-14 years is 1.06 per cent higher than the female children of the average total population which is because of high rate of female infanticide among the majority community, especially among higher castes. This is more clear when we see the comparative sex-ratio among the children of 0-14 years Muslim 1333, total population 1239 and forward castes 1186 females per 1000 males. This surprising variation in sex ratio is because of bad custom of dowry threat among majority community, particularly among higher castes, which leads to female discrimination to female elimination (infanticide). Dowry is a social evil, which must be eliminated from our society by igniting anti-dowry movement in mass scale.

Sex ratio among working age Muslims is 846, which is quite less than the sex ratio of total and forward caste population, indicates that either young females are not brought to towns from villages or their premature deaths are more or both the factors may be responsible. Similarly old age Muslim males and females are proportionately lower than the total and forward caste population, which indicates that either survival rate among old Muslim is less or they pass their retired lives in villages or both may be applicable. Among Muslims proportions of married men and women are comparatively less than the total and forward males and females, which may be due to poverty or absence of child marriages.

Literacy rate among Muslim males and females is comparatively less by 4.00 to 13.00 per cent than total and forward male and female population. However, the difference among Muslim male and female literacy is not much as difference in total and forward male female literacy. Muslim males and females – High School, Intermediate and B.A. and above pass – are comparatively less than the proportion of total and forward male and female High School, Intermediate and B.A. and above pass by 0.50 to 8.00 percent.

Proportion of male and female students among Muslim population is less by 0.30 to 3.00 per cent than total and forward male and female proportion of students. Muslim male students are only 0.12 per cent higher than their counterpart female students, when this difference is higher among total and forward male and female students, which is 1.80 and 1.99 per cent respectively.

Unemployment among Muslim male working age group (15-59 years) is 13.45 percent, when it is 10.00 per cent among total male working age group. Roughly half of total male population is engaged in one or the other economic activities, may be total, forward or Muslims, but surprisingly in case of females of all social categories are less than 5.00 per cent who are economically engaged.

Out of total employment, Muslim proportion of males and females working as labourers are more than the proportions of males and females to total and forward working as labourers. Similarly, the proportions of Muslim males and females engaged, as artisans are comparatively more than males and females of total and forward engaged as artisans. Muslims males engaged in business are above the average, but their female proportion is less than the average. In government jobs Muslims males are 2.21 per cent while no female was recorded in our survey when among total it is males 6.21 and females 4.14 per cent and among forward males 9.09 and females 8.33 percent, which is clear discrimination. In private jobs Muslims males are below the average, but females are above average.

Muslims occupy comparatively less proportion of pucca houses and more proportion of kutcha houses than the total forward population. Muslims have lowest number of rooms in their houses in comparison to total forward population Muslims occupied houses are proportionately more electrified than the total houses, but quite less than the houses belonging to forward population. Muslim occupied houses are proportionately more with latrines within the campus than the average houses, but still less than the houses belonging to forward population. However, the proportions of latrines in Muslim houses are less with but more are dry (service latrines) in comparison to houses belonging to total and forward population. Muslim occupied houses with bathrooms within the campus are proportionately bit more than the average houses but less than the houses with bathrooms belonging to forward population. Muslim houses with source of drinking water are almost equal to proportion of average houses with source of drinking water but quite less than the houses belonging to forward population.

By summing up the above conclusion one can observe that overall Muslims in urban areas are socially and economically below the average and quite behind the forward caste population, which needs special attention in government policies.

5

A STUDY OF THE HEALTH STATUS OF MUSLIM WOMEN IN INDIA

— M. Muzammil

Health means life. It is a relative term. Complete possession of health is an ideal never achieved and entire absence of health means death. Greater possession of health is the goal the achievement of which is always sought for. Good health and poor health are thus only relative positions. With increasing social awareness, concerns for health is growing and spreading very fast.

With emphasis on human development in the decade of 1990s, health became an important ingredient in the measurement of human development. Women's health came to occupy important place in gender-related development indices. Health influences the development of the human individual and the society in many ways. This is the reason that health has been assigned so much significance in the process of economic, social and human development. Even religiously speaking, from the view point of Islam, health of the human individual is of such paramount value that even compulsory religious duties are set aside.

Health is vital to every individual. It is surely more important for women from several considerations. Foremost is the fact that their health ensures the health of children who make the future of any nation. Women in general themselves are a deprived lot therefore their health speaks of the healthy status of the society.

Often it is believed that Muslims are an economically and socially backward community in India and their women are relatively more deprived. But a look at the tables of data generated by the National Family and Health Survey (NFHS) 1998-99 reveals that in most of the indicators of health (viz. food, nutrition, child care and health awareness), the status of Muslim women is relatively better than their counterparts in the majority community and those in other minority communities.

This paper makes an enquiry into this spectacular revelation of the NFHS. It examines various aspects of the health of Muslim women, their relative weaknesses and areas of strengths. It also explores the potentialities for further improvement in the health of Muslim women.

The Concept of Health

Health implies more than the absence of sickness in the human individual. It indicates a state of harmonious functioning of the body and mind in relation to the physical and social environment. Good health enables the individual to enjoy life to the fullest possible extent and to reach the maximum level of productive capacity.

With regard to women in general, health is an illusive concept. It is defined as the complete possession of physical, mental, social and spiritual well being. Often life expectancy at birth (average age) is taken as proxy for the status of health just as literacy rate is generally adopted for education.

Lack of adequate food supply and nutrition, combined

with rudimentary health facilities, leads to low life expectancy and high mortality. Conversely, better food consumption and the intake of nutrients often ensure better health. Viewed from this angle Muslim women, on the whole, are better placed than their counterparts in the majority community. However, there are certain areas of concern which need attention and remedy.

Food Consumption

Consumption of food and nutritious diet is important for women's health. Adequate amounts of protein, fat, carbohydrates, vitamins and minerals are required for a well balanced diet. The NFHS examined he consumption of the following items of food:

- Milk and curd
- Pulses or beans
- Green, leafy vegetables
- Other vegetables
- Fruits
- Eggs
- Chicken, meat or fish

Among the above listed seven items of food, Muslim women are found to be better placed in as many as five as compared to their Hindu counterparts. In the consumption only of milk and pulses, Muslim women are relatively worse off. These facts are borne out by figures given in Table 1.

Nutritional Status

Height and body mass index (BMI) are supposed to be the outcome of nutritional diet during the childhood and adolescence. A woman's height is often used to identify women at risk of having a difficult delivery, since small stature is usually related to small pelvic size. The risk of having a baby with low birth weight is also higher for mothers who are short.

TABLE 1

Percentage of Ever Married Women Consuming Specific Food at Least once a Week

Type of Food	*Hindu Women*	*Muslim Women*
Milk or curd	55.7	46.8
Pulses or beans	88.5	83.7
Green, leafy veg.	85.1	85.8
Other vegetables	93.0	93.8
Fruits	31.9	32.9
Eggs	24.9	44.1
Chicken, meat or fish	27.5	55.7

Source: NFHS data.

Natural height of women varies among different groups of population. The cut-off point for height, below which a woman can be identified as nutritionally at risk is usually in the range of 140-150 centimeters. The mean height for women in India is 151cms. Related data for Muslim women are given in Table 2.

Table 2 indicates that Muslim women are found to be marginally better both from the view point of mean height and the body mass index (BMI). The BMI is an index which relates a woman's height to her weight. It can be used to assess both thinness and obesity. The BMI excludes the pregnant women and the nursing mothers of two months. The BMI of 18.5 value is of great significance. Chronic energy deficiency is usually indicated by a BMI of less than 18.5. Larger percentage of women below this level indicates of high prevalence of nutritional deficiency.

TABLE 2

Height and Body Mass Index of Women

Specification	*Hindu*	*Muslim Women*
Mean height (cms.)	151.1	151.5
Percentage of women below 145 cms.	13.5	12.3
Mean body mass index (BMI)	20.1	20.5
Percentage of women below BMI 18.5 kg/m^2	36.9	34.1

Source: Same as in Table 1.

Note: The body mass index (BMI) is the ratio of the weight in kilograms to the square of height in meters (kg/m^2)

In other works, nutritional status shows the physical fitness,which in turn ensures mental health.

Nutritional Deficiency

Nutritional deficiency among women results into anemia, which is characterized by a low level of hemoglobin in the blood. Hemoglobin is necessary for transporting oxygen from lungs to other tissues and organs of the body. The youthfulness of the individual depends on the chemistry of blood. Women usually suffer from iron deficiency in blood. The position of Muslim women, in this regard, is found to be relatively better.

Data related with the position of anaemia among the Muslim women are given in Table 3 which shows that Muslim women are fond to be less anaemia in all the three categories of anaemia – mild, moderate and severe, as compared to their counterparts in the majority community.

TABLE 3

Percentage of Ever Married Women Having Iron Deficiency Anaemia by Degree of Anaemia

Description	*Hindu Women*	*Muslim Women*
Women with any anaemia	52.4	49.6
Women with mild anaemia	35.5	34.2
Women with moderate anaemia	15.0	14.2
Women with severe anaemia	2.0	1.3

Source: Same as in Table 1.

Anaemia or iron deficiency is the most wide – spread form of malnutrition among women. Anaemia is also a serious health problem.

Health of Children

The health of children and childcare are very closely related with the health of the mother. In vaccination of children under three years of age, the percentage of Muslim is relatively better both in case of vaccination from the public sector and vaccination through the private medical sector. In vitamin A supplementation etc. however, Muslim children are adversely placed as compared to their counterparts in the majority community.

Muslim children are found to be suffering more from diseases like cough, fever and diarrhoea. Interestingly, Muslim women are relatively more aware of the remedy i.e. oral dehydration salt (ORS) than their counterparts in the majority community. Relatively larger percentage of Muslim women take the suffering children to a health facility provider.

Data pertaining to childhood vaccination of Muslim children is given in Table 4. It provides information about the following vaccinations:

- BCG
- Polio (O)
- DPT (three doses)
- Polio (three doses)
- Measles.

The table shows that in case of BCG vaccination 62.3 percentage of Muslim children in the age group of 12-23 months are covered as against 72.5 per cent children in the Hindu community.

TABLE 4

Percentage of Children Age 12-23 Months Who Received Specific Vaccinations at Any Time

Type of vaccination	*Hindu*	*Muslim*
BCG	72.5	62.3
Polio O	13.1	9.9
DPT		
1	72.1	63.2
2	65.6	56.0
3	55.7	45.7
Polio		
1	84.7	76.3
2	79.3	70.0
3	63.5	54.0
Measles	51.5	40.4
All *	42.4	32.7
None	13.3	21.0
Vaccination card holders	33.7	30.6

Source: Same as in Table 1

* Includes BCG, measles, three dozes each of DPT and Polio (excluding Polio 0).

Table 4 depicts the disadvantageous position of the

children of Muslim community though their women are relatively better placed from several indicators of health as given earlier. It points towards increased negligence and carelessness of Muslim women in bringing up of their children. It is also a reflection on the poverty of Muslim families.

Awareness of HIV/AIDS

Muslim women are relatively behind in their knowledge about AIDS – the illness which is caused by HIV virus. It weakens the immune system and leads to death through secondary infections such as tuberculosis and pneumonia etc.

The position of Muslim women about their source of knowledge of AIDS is given in Table 5 which shows that they are lesser aware of this disease.

TABLE 5

Source of Knowledge About AIDS: Percentage of Who Have Heard of AIDS from Specific Sources

Source of knowledge	*Hindu women*	*Muslim women*
Percentage who have heard about AIDS	39.2	35.4
Radio	42.3	37.2
Television	79.8	75.0
Cinema	8.7	4.9
News-paper/magazines	26.0	23.5
Poster/hoarding	12.4	8.4
Health worker	3.5	2.9
Adult education programmme	0.4	0.7
Friend/relative	30.7	30.0
School teacher	1.0	1.1
Other sources	6.6	3.1

Source: same as in Table 1

Table 5 reveals that though the awareness of Muslim women about AIDS is less as compared to Hindu women, the difference is not substantial.

Conclusion

The following points emerge from the analysis of NFHS sample survey data in India:

- The health status of Muslim women in India, in general, is not poor.
- In many respects, Muslim women are far better than their counterparts in the majority community.
- In areas where Muslim women are lagging behind, their backwardness is only marginal.
- Education and awareness about health related issues is relatively less among the Muslim women.
- Health of the Muslim children is found to be relatively poor.
- The better health status of the mother is less reflected in the child.
- The findings suggest that perhaps negligence and resourcelessness are the main causes of the poor health of their children.
- Exposure to mass media about health awareness is not very low among Muslim women. It points towards a positive social change among them.
- There is not much difference in the behaviour pattern of the Muslim women as compared to their counterparts in the majority community in the treatment of illness.
- Vaccination drives have reached the Muslim women/mothers but the coverage of their

children is still less than the average for the majority community.

Policy Implications

Several policy implications flow from the foregoing analysis. The composition of consumption needs to be changed for still better results on the health front. Consumption of milk and milk products and that of pulses and beans needs to be encouraged among the Muslim women as they are lagging behind in these respects.

The prevalence of anaemia needs to be attended carefully because it not only affects the present generation but also the future generation. Anaemia results in an increased risk of premature delivery and low birth weight. Early detection of anaemia can help prevent complications related to pregnancy and delivery, as well as child development problems. Full information needs to be made available about the extent of anaemia in order that iron fortification programme is improved. The provision of iron and folic acid tablets to the pregnant women under the Government of India's Reproductive and Child Health Programme needs to be made more effective so that pregnancy anaemia is prevented and health of the future children is better ensured.

Health awareness of women needs to be increased through health oriented education. The use of mass media can be very effective and useful in this regard.

Resourcelessness of women often comes in the way of the treatment of their illness and that of their children. The dependence on public health facility is still very large among the Muslim families, care must be taken that it is not adversely affected while 'redefining the role of the government' under the second generation reform programme.

6

POLITICAL PARTCIPATION OF MUSLIM WOMEN—'A MINORITY WITH A MINORITY'

— *Shashi Shukla*

Muslim women constitute a 'minority within a minority' in two sense. One, as a minority within a religious minority i.e. Indian Muslims and two, ad a minority with a political minority i.e., Indian women.

It may be state at the outset that the Muslim women do not form a homogenous group. There is a divisions among them, both vertical and horizontal, based on their socio-economic status, urban / rural residence, region, sect, traditional school of jurisprudence and customary laws. However, despite heterogeneity two feature shared by all Muslim women are their gender and their minority status. Muslim women are as much affected by the socio-economic, political situation facing the Muslim community in India as those facing the Indian Women as a whole.

It is an irony that Muslim women have been accorded an equal status with men, by the Holy Quran as well as by Indian Constitution, but the equality of status in principle has not been actualised in practice.

Equality of rights, it may be pointed out, is meaningless without equal access to rights. This brings into focus the relevance of political participation of Muslim women as participation in political life is integral to the whole problem of advancement of Muslim women. No enduring solution to the Muslim community's most threatening social, economic and political problems can be found with out full participation and political empowerment of Muslim women.

The paper focuses on three relevant themes of Muslim women's political participation namely nature of participation, factor affecting the participation and measures required to enhance the participation.

Political participation is an ingredient of political process. International Encyclopedia of Social Science defines political participation as, "those voluntary activities by which members of the society shares the selection of rulers and directly and indirectly in the formation of public policy.[1] Hence, every political system, more so democracies presume the participation of women along with the men in the political activities.[2] Democracies recognise men and women as equal partners in the shaping and sharing of political power. As women constitute one half of the human population, their political participation assumes great significance. Political participation means not merely exercising the franchise but also co-decision making and co-policy making at all levels of government. There can be no gender equality without such kind of participation.

Politics associated with power has been traditionally considered a male preserve. The bulk of empirical research indicates that compared to men, women's formal political participation is less. The participation of women in politics is found to be declining as one moves towards more active kind of participation especially in political leadership and goverment.[3] It is a global phenomenon, Indian being no exception. However, the participation of Muslim women in India has been reported even much lesser as compared to that of the non-Muslim women.[4] Apart from the gender factor the Muslim women face many more constraints on their participation as members of religious minority community that is both, educationally and socio-economically backward, and culturally orthodox and conservative.

Nature of Participation

The association of Indian women with politics goes back to the pre-independence days when they participated in the various phases of the freedom struggle as volunteers, leaders and commanders[5] and suffered like men.[6] Such participation could be possible due to the spade work done by the social and religious reformers in the field of women's education emancipation and uplift. These reforms paved in the way for an Indian Women's Movement within the Indian National Movement. Women's participation increased manifold as the national movement acquired a mass character under the leadership of Mahatma Gandhi.

The approach of the Muslim social reformers was slightly different. The community had distanced itself from the main stream after 1857 Revolt and was in grip of intellectual decay, traditionalism and conservatism. The emphasis of the reform was on reinterpreting the Islamic tenets to show that Islam was neither antithetical to the minority status nor too western education.[7] The aim was educational upliftment and emancipation of Muslim men.

Yet the zeal for reforms, particularly the emphasis on education, did benefit some Muslim women. The educated Muslim women with their exposure to the outside world and growing awareness organized themselves in the course of time and worked towards the betterment of the Muslim women.

A Muslim Women Movement was launched, which in the course of time allied itself with the Indian Women's Movement. Some women went beyond participating for the cause of the Muslim women, and volunteered themselves for involvement in the Indian Freedom Struggle, thus committing themselves to the national cause. Among the politically active Muslim women were Bi Amma, Amjadi Begum, Begum Hasrat, Mohani, Amina and Rehana Tayabji, Begum Sakina Luqmani, Fatima Ismael and Heero. A. Ahmadi.[8]

Bi Amma, the mother of Ali brothers, was a part of the delegation that met Lord Montague in 1917 under Mrs. Sarojini Naidu regarding the enfranchisement of Indian women. Begum Shahnawaz, Begum Aijaz Rasool and Begum Ikramullah were among the fourteen women members of the Constituent Assembly when it met in December 1946.

However, unlike the Hindu women who participated enmasse in the National movement, the participation among the Muslim women was confined to an elite class. The reasons for the limited participation could be attributed to both, the traditional factors like of purdah and segregation among the Muslim as well as to the Muslim separatist politics which is dominated the Indian political scene from 1920 to 1947.[9] Besides, The Muslim League did not encompass masses and as such the Muslim women were denied the opportunity to participate in the National Movment.[10] The mobilization of the women was undertaken by the Muslim League after 1935.

Muslim women's cause suffered with the country's partition, the migration of Muslim women leaders, and the passage of the Hindu Code Bill and the Muslim community's minority status in independent India.[11]

The constitution of the free India modelled largely after the constitutions of western liberal democracies, where universal adult franchise and equal constitutional rights for women had been recognized, and more important in recognition of the contribution made by the women towards India's freedom, accorded equal status to them by way of granting equal rights.

However, the assumption that political rights would automatically take care of women's problems, their upliftment and development, has not come true. Political rights have not empowered the Indian women, including the Muslim women.

The election statistics indicate a general trend of increase in voting turn out, of Muslim women. But their active political participation has been reported low.[12]

The number of Muslim women members has never gone beyond three in Lok Sabha. The ninth, tenth and eleventh Lok Sabha did not have any Muslim representation. Uttar Pradesh, the most populous state of Indian union and having a sizeable population of the Muslim also presents a dismal picture. The Muslim women's representation in State Vidhan Sabha has never crossed the mark of two. Although there has been the increase in the number of Muslim women contestants, yet the actual number of women, who have been elected, has been very low. There was absolutely no Muslim women representation in the second, fourth, eleventh, twelfth and thirteenth Vidhan Sabha.[13] It is interesting to note two facts about the Muslim women's candidature. One, the Muslim political parties have not fielded or returned any Muslim women to the

Vidhan Sabha. Two, roughly one half of the Muslim women contested the elections as independent candidates, for they failed to get the party nomination.[14]

The nature and pattern of political participation of Muslim women is found to be not much different from that of the non-Muslim women, in the sense that the overall participation of women is more in spectator activities which require less time, energy and initiative for participation. The participation goes down in the transitional activities and further down in the gladiatorial activities. However, what is striking about the Muslim women is the smallness of their numbers and percentage especially in the transitional and gladiatorial activities. Also striking is the fact that there is no correlation between the number of Muslim women, their voting percentage and representation.

It may be stated that by and large the Muslim women stand at a low level of political participation.

Factors Affecting the Participation

Muslim women's political participation can be understood in three perspectives-gender, minority and Islamic. In addition to the psychological, situational and structural factors which account for week participation of women in general, the Muslim women participation is affected by special factors peculiar to their situation, namely the minority and the Islamic Factor.

Although Muslims are the largest minority group, yet compared to other minorities, they are an insecure minority, gripped by a fear psychosis-a product of India's partition days. Moin Shakir writes, "What Muslims got out of partition was a sense of insecurity, frustration, and uncertainity.[15] This has given rise to the minority psyche leading to their alienation and withdrawal from the national imaginary[16] and adversely affected the community.

Muslims are not only an insecure but also the most backward community in educational and socio- economic terms.[17] The British rule and this trend continued even after the attainment of independence. Consequently, they remain under-represented in the educational institutions, legislatures and services. Their representation in government is less than their proportion in the population.

The community's weak political, social and economic position in the society seriously affects the status of Muslim women as there exists a close correlation between the two.

The community is not only educationally and economically backward but also religiously orthodox and culturally conservative. Religiosity is relatively of greater degree among Muslim than among the other communities.[19]

The religious orthodoxy, cultural conservatism and desire for a distinct cultural identify has been in particular unfavorable and unfair to the women as they are perceived as the symbols of Muslim Identity. Consequently, they are subjected to many restrictive social and cultural norms.

Islam was the first religion to accept women as a legal entity and accord her rights in the matters of marriage, divorce, maintenance etc. The holy Quran lays down that her obligation equals her rights.[20] Islam evolved a progressive status for women and women like Khazia, Bibi Ayesha, Bibi Fatima, Zubaida and Buran actively participated in public affairs.[21] The Islamic society, however, became feudalized after the death of Prophet Muhammad.[22] The women lost their position under the partriarchal values upheld by the feudal society. The fedual attitude towards women through corresponding interpretation of the *Quran* during the medieval period came to be thought to have religious sanction.[23]

The Islamic instructions were further diluted in the course of interaction with the other communities. Like in India, Islam was influenced by the dominant Hindu culture particularly in attitudes regarding women. The Muslim women became a victim of socio-cultural irony.[24] The position of Muslim women is influenced by both Islamic injunctions and Hindu tradition. The conservative and restrictive elements of one have tended to dominate or neutralize the liberal elements of the other.[25]

The irony is that now they live in the secular democratic polity where the state freely makes progressive laws for the Hindu women but not for their Muslim counterparts, who continue to be governed by the Muslim Personal Law. Shad Bano Ahamad says, "a secular Indian State, over conscious about the privileges and rights of Muslims did not dare to take liberties with the sentiment of the minorities."[26]

In the absence of any Muslim leader of nation wide following or any national political party of Muslim, the leadership of the community rests in the hands of religious leaders who oppose any reforms in the Muslim Personal Law, to maintain their hold over the masses. The whole question of change in the Muslim Personal Law has become identity related[27] and the desire for a distinct identity has been particularly unfavourable to the women.[28]

Conclusion

It may be stated that with the spread of education and process of modernization, a change has occurred in the social position of Muslim women. However, the overall situation is not very satisfactory. According to many studies, the Muslim women are still among the most backward section of the society.

Education, both secular and religious, is the key word to the progress of Muslim women. Th positive impact of education on the lives and status of Muslim women has been highlighted in various studies.[29]

Muslim Personal Law as it stands today is anti-women and discriminatory against them. It urgently requires change but it is better if the initiative is taken by the community itself.[30] There ought to be a feminist theological perception of the subject i.e. interpretation of the *Quran* from the women's point of view.

Muslim Personal Law needs reform but the issue should not be politicized, what is important is not to harp on this issue alone but to concentrate on real issues-universalization of primary education, adult education, vocational training, better health and hygiene, family planning guidance, economic self-reliance and equal pay for equal work. There must be a specific government policy designed for Muslim women, Keeping in view their needs, problems, interests, and priorities.

Apart from the state responsibility in this matter, the responsibility also lies on the shoulders of women's organisation and political parties.

Since self-help is the best help, an organized movement among the Muslim women is the need of the hour. A movement which raises Muslim women oriented issues and works towards their capacity building.

A more meaningful and positive role on the part of Muslim women leaders is also required. They must cut across party lines to work for the empowerment of Muslim women.

The media should also pay a more constructive role.

Instead of projecting the stereo-type image of Muslim women, they should focus on successful Muslim women working in different walks f life, who have risen above their situation, without giving up their traditional culture and values.

The attitudinal change is equally important among the Muslim men. However, more than a change in societal attitude towards women, what is desired is a change in self-perception of Muslim women. The capacity building of Muslim women is a must to escape the destiny of "a minority within a minority" and to emerge as an empowered being, with a well defined status and identity.

REFERENCES

1. Herbet McClosky, "Political Participation" in *International Encyclopedia of Social Sciences,* Vol. 12, MacMillan, New York, 1968, p. 252.
2. See, Gabriel Almond and Sidney Verba, *The Civic Culture,* Princeton University Press, New Jersey, 1963; N.D. Palmer, *Elections and Political Development; The South Asian Experience,* Vikas Publishing House, New Delhi, 1976.
3. See, Maurice Duverger, *The Political Role of Women,* UNESCO, Paris, 1955; Vicky Randall, *Women and Politics,* MacMillan, London, 1989.
4. Sushila Jain, "Political Awareness and Political Commitment: A Study of Muslim Women in Jaipur City", *Paper presented at the Second National Conference on Women's Studies,* Kerala University, Trivendrum, April 9-12, 1984.
5. V. Rajalakshmi, *Political Behaviour of Women in Tamil Nadu,* Inter India Publications, New Delhi, 1985, p. 19.
6. Manmohan Kaur, *Role of Women in the Freedom Movement 1857-1947,* Sterling Publishers, New Delhi, 1968, pp. 63-64.
7. Shahida Lateef, *Muslim Women in India: Political and Private Realities, 1890s-1980s,* Kali For Women, New Delhi, 1990, p. 76.
8. Uma Vasudev, "Women in Politics", in Z. Siddiqui and A.

Zuberi (eds.) *Muslim Women: Problems and Prospects,* M.D. Publishing Pvt. Ltd., New Delhi, 1993, p. 75.

9. Shahida Lateef, n. 3, p. 94.
10. Shad Bano Ahmed, "Methodological Problems in the Study of Muslim Women", in Mohini Anjum (ed.) *Muslim Women in India*, Radiant Publishers, New Delhi, 1992, p. 30.
11. Shahida Lateef, n. 3, p. 74.
12. Zanab Babu, "Political Status of Muslim Women", *The U.P. Journal of Political Sciences,* Vol. 2, No. 1, Jan.-June 1990, pp. 307-46.
13. Results of the General Election to the U.P. Vidhan Sabha, Election Directorate, Uttar Pradesh.
14. U.P. Vidhan Sabha, *Who is Who? From 1952 to 1991.*
15. Moin Shakir, *Muslims in Free India,* Kalamkar Prakashan, New Delhi, 1972, p. 1.
16. V.V. Saiyed and Sarojini Narain, "Problems of Education of Muslim Women in Delhi", in Siddiqui and Zuberi (eds.) *Muslim Women: Problems and Prospects,* p. 109.
17. 55% of Muslim are below poverty line, whereas the growth rate of the community is 3.3%, literacy is less than 40%.
18. M.M. Siddiqui, "Muslim Backwardness – An Analysis", *The Times of India,* June 13, 1993.
19. Talat Ara Asharafi, *Muslim Women in Changing Perspectives,* Commonwealth Publications, New Delhi, 1992, p. 3.
20. Asghar Ali Engineer, "The Reality about Muslim Women", *The Times of India,* December 22, 1993.
21. Zeenat Shaukat Ali, "Women in Islam", in Siddiqui and Zuberi (eds.) *Muslim Women: Problems and Prospects,* pp. 22-23.
22. Asghar Ali Engineer, "Social Dynamics and Status of Women in Islam" in Sushila Agarwal (ed.) *Status of Women,* Printwell Publishers, Jaipur, 1988, p. 75.
23. *Ibid.,* p. 75.
24. A.R. Saiyed, "Muslim Women in India: An over view", in Mohini Anjun (ed.) *Muslim Women in India,* p. 3.
25. Zarina Bhatty, "Socio-Economic Status of Muslim Women", in Siddiqui and Zuberi (eds.) *Muslim Women: Problems and Prospects,* p. 13.

26. Shad Bano Ahmed, n. 6, p. 28.
27. Urooji Abid and M.G. Hussain, "Problems of Muslim Women", *Mainstream,* February 12, 1994, p. 15.
28. Zarina Bhatty, n. 21.
29. See, Shibani Roy, *Status of Muslim Women in North India,* B.R. Publishers, Delhi, 1978; M. Indu Menon, *Status of Muslim Women in India: A Case Study of Kerala,* Uppal Publishing House, New Delhi, 1981.
30. Sakina Hasan, "The Status of Muslim Women", *Seminar* 416, April 1994, p. 27.

7

STRUGGLE OF MUSLIM WOMEN AGAINST ORTHODOX SOCIAL ORDER

—Dr. Ramesh Madan

Women for centuries have been geared into second class roles in a general patriarchal Society throughout the world. There was some change in the role and status of women everywhere by the end of the second world war and more so with the declaration of International Women's Year and the decade thereafter plus the Beijing Conference has had remarkable impact on the perception and motivation of women irrespective of religion, caste, culture and ethnicity.

The basic contention of this paper is to examine the struggle of Muslim women in getting rid of orthodox social order. Therefore, some of the questions raised would veer around How do Muslim women in India perceive the UN declaration of elimination of all forms of discrimination against women. Also, whether these and other forces change have enabled their participation in various socio-economic and political activities in the socio-economic and political scenario of our country? If no, than will Universal civil code in case enforced be helpful? Will it or not help Muslim women change their legal status? In case the Muslim women incorporate and fight for their socio-economic rights what will be the reaction of various schools of thought? Will they approve or reject women's adoption to the change? Muslim women, themselves a minority within a minority- will they hinder up taking up these challenges of changing scenario? Still even today, in India among many of the debate on Muslim women and gender has revolved around on 'Islamic Fundamentalism' as propounded by the religious leaders especially the Ulema and other theologians. In fact, historically from religious orthodoxy. Especially since the predicament of the Shah Bano's case, Muslim women's role in the Indian society is being debated now & than.

The Shahbano controversy has led to faction between Muslim women themselves as it saw the entry of heavily veiled women in public who denounced the court's judgement and projected themselves as defenders of Islam.

In conclusion, despite the backwardness of Muslim women throughout the world, in India as well as elsewhere, a small segment of Muslim population have begun to perceive the relevance of education and employment necessary for the empowerment of Muslim women. Thus, Muslim girls are being encouraged by the parents, community and NGO's to seek higher education in all fields including professional. This has led to their entrance into the fields other than unorganized sector, on the one hand, has resulted in some change from Tradition to modernity in the positive sense; on the other hand, it means conflict between liberal Muslims and Fundamentalists. A few groups among the fundamentalists have even taken the help of the gun, as in the Kashmir Valley, in Hyderabad and elsewhere demanding purdah. With these developments on the Indian subcontinent, it may be argued that still mass mobilization is required for the improvement in the status of India Muslim women.

Unless and until women themselves are united or change their attitude nothing concrete can be done or is possible.

Moreover, Globalization is bringing with it values of Western Culture and these are vitally effecting the Muslim world but it is still possible that they can hold to their culture for quite sometime unless some possibility of reform is initiated for equality of Muslim women with their other sisters in the non-Muslim world. This realization is already there in many parts of the Muslim world and of recent there was a procession in Morocco where lakhs of people supported gender equality.

8

MUSLIM WOMEN AND LEGAL EMBEDDEDNESS

—*Vaishali Saxena*

Present age is age of laws. State determines *model code of conduct for citizens and govern their lives through laws.* Hence, a *legal system* is a *system of governance and control*. But more over, it is a *'system of communication'*. It communicates rights and duties of the citizens and institutions as it encompasses provisions relating with it. It prescribes do's and don'ts of state and individual's behaviour. So it is also a system of determining legitimacy of individual and state's action / non-action. But above all it is a *system of justice.* These laws are like guardians, promoting harmony, growth and development of the society. Consequently a fair legal system, complex free, accessible to all, cost effective is a necessary corollary of growth of the individuals and the state.

Individuals are embedded in various powerful overlapping institutions like community, caste, place of work, religion etc. These institutions have distinct values and beliefs. Sometimes they stimulate and reinforce each other's value; sometimes they stand apart with conflicting values. If state bypasses these embeddedness and communicate directly may overlook opportunities for influence over target behaviour and may be vulnerable to counter pressures mediating from these institutions. But danger in encompassing these embeddedness is conflict in their values as they overlap and have different dimensions. Legal environment around Muslim women emanates from religious, social, political and judicial institutions. Indian constitutions, Muslim Personal, law, Indian Judicial system have political, religious and legal dimensions. Inevitably their merger inherits dilemmas and conflicts.

A constitution of the country is a legal code of nation's conduct. The constitution is highest law of the nation. Indian constitution, which was promulgated on 26 January 1950, protects interests of the citizens. Constitution has made provisions of Fundamental rights and Directive Principles. Citizens are safe guarded through these provisions. The constitution has treated man, woman equal, submits equality before law and prohibits discrimination on the grounds of caste, religion, gender etc.

Muslim Personal Law: The British legal principles and notions of justice influenced the Indian existing judicial system and administration of justice as early, as the beginning of the 17th century. The trading East India Company began to exercise responsibility, until 1665, was limited only to the factories belonging to the Company. Subsequent establishment of three High Courts in 1861 opened a meaningful judicial chapter and the British adopted it as the part and parcel of the law of the land.

The British applied the Islamic legal principles to the Muslim community as a matter of administrative policy. They allowed the Muslims to continue to be governed by their personal laws. This permission assumed a statutory status under the provisions of the charter of George II granted in 1753, where by the Muslim could obtain exemption from the Mayor's court to get their cases adjudicated on the basis of their personal laws. Virtually the non-interference in the personal laws of other communities was not a British innovation. The study of the history of administration of justice reveals that British India inherited from the Mughal administration of justice. It did not force its own notion of law on the people, and to accept the principles that each religious community was entitled to profess its own religion and to obey its own law. The British were convinced of feasibility of this policy which came to be reiterated by the Mufassil regulation 1772, promulgated during the time of Warren Hastings, and later enacted as section 27 of the Regulation of 1780 which provided:

> "That in all suits regarding the inheritance, marriage and cases, and other religious usages and institutions, the laws of the Koran with respect to Mohammedans and where only one of the parties shall be Mohammedan the laws and usages of the defendant should invariably be adhered to."

Again as back as 1937 the British legislatures reassured the determination of Muslim Personal law through the application of Shariat. Section 2 of the Muslim Personal law (Shariat) Application Act XXVI 1937 provides.

> "Notwithstanding any custom or usages to the contrary, in all questions (save question relating to agricultural land) regarding intestate succession, special property of females, including personal property inherited or obtained under contract or gift or any other provision of personal law, marriage, dissolution, including talaq, ila, zihar, khula, mubarat, maintenance, dower guardianship, gift, trusts, and trust properties

> and waqfs (other than charities and charitable institutions and religious endorsements) the rule of decision in cases where the parties are Muslims shall be the Muslim personal law (Shariat)."

From the ongoing one may conclude that Muslim Personal law draws heavily from religion, legitimized by the state. Data given Table 1 suggests that despite its partly religious nature, illiterate women (Muslim) are largely unaware about it.

TABLE 1

Educational Status of Muslim Women and Muslim Personal Law[1]

	Education Status of the Muslim Women	
Level of Awareness	*Literate %*	*Illiterate %*
Aware	92.96	13.33
Not Aware	7.04	86.67

1. Data is extracted from unpublished Ph.D. Thesis by Saba Tabassum titled "Muslim Women in Indian Constitution", Lucknow University, 1992.

Muslim Personal laws are legal forms of the customs, urges and traditions found from ancient days in the form of Shariat, prevalent in Muslim society. Family affairs, property matters, marriage, divorce have been settled on the basis of shariat rules, Shariat is code of conduct for Muslims, main source of it is *Quran*. Let us now examine some interesting data in this regard. (1) Islam bestows all kind of rights on Muslim women including right to property. But data suggested that only 33% cases it was available to her and 77% it was non-available. (2) Shariat has made provisions of verbal divorce. Simple pronouncement of divorce three times does not revoke duly solemnized marriage. Data regarding acceptance of verbal divorce among Muslim women cogently refused it as a system of divorce as 56% respondents show non-acceptance. Further in religious form of divorce is more popular with the 83.12% than the divorce through court. Study also concluded that 57.34% respondents agreed to bring change in some provision of the Shariat. 42.56% were against towards such changes and 55.82% preferred change in divorce procedure. Changes in provisions of maintenance were preferred by 54%.

Highly debated and widely publicized case of Shah Bano Begum ruled the provisions of Muslim law regarding maintenance of a divorced wife and granted the same under the section of 125 of Cr.P.C.

The case (AIR 1985, S.C. 119), with Mohammed Ahmed Khan as appellant and Shah Bano Begum and others as respondents, relates to Sections 125 and 127 (1) of the Criminal Procedure Code, which provides maintenance for divorced women. Mr. Mohammed Ahmed Khan who is a lawyer by profession, was married to Shah Bano Begum in 1932. Three sons and two daughters were from that marriage. Mr. Khan contracted a second marriage in 1946, of which six children were born. In 1975 he drove Shah Bano Begum out of his house. In April 1978, she filed a petition against her husband under section 125 of the Cr.P.C. in the court of the Judicial Magistrate, Indore, asking for maintenance at the rate of Rs. 500/- per month, on November 6, 1978. Mr. Khan divorced his wife by irrevocable triple talaq in August 1979 the magistrate directed Mr. Khan to pay a sum of Rs. 25 per month to Shah Bano Begum by way of maintenance.

Stating the judgement in Shah Bano case, delivered on May 23, 1985 Mr. Justice Y.V. Chandrachud observed that section 125 is the part of the Code of Criminal procedure and this admits no distinction on the religion. In fact it cuts across the boundaries of religion. Further clause (B) of the explanation of section 125 (I) which defines 'wife' including 'divorced wife' applicable to all women including Muslim women. Therefore, 'divorced' Muslim women so long not married is wife for the purpose of sections 125. In other words, section 125 overrides personal law.

Even during the British administration of justice, it was often experienced allegedly that in some situations Islamic Law failed to offer a definite legal principle with the common law or that indigenous rule was so old and unsuited to the needs of a rapidly developing society, in such circumstances some principles for doing some substantial justice had to be enunciated. Hence study concludes that Indian Constitution partially protects the rights of the Muslim women. Courts often settled the dispute on the assumption which negated the basic postulates of Islamic Law. Sometimes the well-settled doctrine of English Law made in roads which disturbed the principles of Muslim law. Some times judicial interpretative elasticity distorted and restricted the Muslim law and emphasized social justice, social change and dynamism in reformative social revolution even at the cost of expressed provisions of Islamic law. Sometimes the court viewed that Islamic law being immutable and could not satisfy the needs of a changing and growing society. Further major Islamic principles of Muslim Personal law are based on god made laws and man-made laws can not change its basics.

Whenever these institutions enter into each other's domain and collide, it is followed by war of supremacy and power testing, resulting in hostility for each other, and leaving citizen's gasping. In Agha Mohammed vs. Kulsoombee case it was observed: "...It would be wrong for the courts on the point of this kind to put their own construction of *Quran* in opposition to the express ruling of the commentators of such great antiquity and high authority." I propose these laws must be progressive in nature keeping temporal dimension in context and only serviceable criteria to determine their correctness should be their capacity to impart justice. Then only we would be able to cut across all gender-related barriers and progress towards equality.

Wills, legacies and adoption. There is no uniformatics, and justification to keep the law in its present state. Legislature alone can remedy this defect.

9

THE MUSLIM-MINORITY FACTOR IN INDIA'S POLITICAL ECONOMY: A RELATIVE GROWTH ANALYSIS

—S.P. Mishra

Not much is known about the Economics of Minorities in India. Whatever studies are there, they lack a comprehensive framework to enable the policy makers and interested parties to make a relative growth analysis. Therefore, a relative growth framework is needed to analyse the performance of India's political economy during the post-Independence period by taking into account the *Muslim-minority factor* which has been changing its position for political parties which proclaimed to cater better to serve the Muslim-minority interests. A summary review of 50 years of planning in India reveals that the relative growth pattern has not adequately benefited the poor and the under-privileged, in general and the minorities, in particular. The Congress Government and even the coalition Governments in the centre which have come into power in between and afterwards, including the present NDA Government, have been constantly impressing upon the people of India that the Indian system of planning aims at building a socialist, or socialistic pattern of society. The Governments have been proclaiming measures to achieve growth with social justice, removal of poverty, removal of exploitation and inequality of incomes. But then, it is not slogans or political catch phrases the matter. The more relevant thing is we as a nation is moving forward in the right direction or not.

The crucial question, in the historical context, is: whether the lot of the underdog, the weak and the under-privileged has improved? In other words, have the benefits of development percolated down to the lower layers of Indian society or have they been appropriated by a small group of the rich and the higher-middle classes? It is the contention of many economists and political observers that the poor in India have not really benefited from economic planning and that, to a large extent, the rich has became richer while the vast majority of the poor have remained hopelessly poor. The philosophical foundations of the planning process in India were sound but there have been crisis after crisis at the level of implementation as one American economist has once remarked: *"Indians are good planners, but bad executors"*. In this respect, I am of the firm view that growth should be treated not only *as ends* but also *as means* to achieve certain other socio-economic objectives to lead a peaceful co-existence for all the communities and to ensure *growth of all the people, growth by all the people and growth for all the people.*

Having this framework in mind, an attempt has been made in this paper to apply and analyse various indicators of relative growth in the case of minorities in relation to majority social groups. An exercise has also been made to analyse the political use of the outcome of the relative growth patterns in Indian economy. Areas of policy concerns have also been indicated at the end of paper.

Indicators of Relative Growth

The ultimate goal of all development efforts is to raise the level of well being of all citizens of our country. Further, analysis of relative growth in India is based on the findings of a multipurpose survey, conducted by the National Council of Applied Economic research (NCAER). New Delhi and commissioned by the Planning Commission, Government of India, in 1994, covering 33,230 households in rural India. For details, see *India Human Development Report, NCAER,* Oxford University Press, 1999. An exercise in the analysis of relative growth should be done not only at all-India level, but also at state level and at social group level to capture the inter-state and inter-community and intra-community differentials. With this end in view, the above survey was spread over 1,765 villages and 195 districts in 16 major states of India including Uttar Pradesh. The following indicators of relative growth of religious groups have been taken into account for further analysis:

- Per capita income
- Literacy rate
- Poverty ratio
- Household income by source
- Amenities available in households
- Gender disparity
- Fertility and mortality rates.

Analysis of Relative Growth

The analysis of relative growth of religious groups is confined to rural households and for the indicators mentioned above as the required data is available only for them. Since the majority of Indian population lives in rural areas, it would not be out of place to mention that the analysis attempted her will be useful for further policy and action. Since independence, India has made significant progress in several areas of development. But a litmus test to ascertain the relative growth performance of Indian economy is to find out how deeply the macro-economic gains have percolate down to the masses.

TABLE 1

Per Capita Income, Literacy Rate and Poverty Ratio Among Religious Groups

Religious Groups	*Per Capita Income (Rs./ Year)*	*Literacy Rate 7+years*	*Population below Poverty line(%)*
Hindus	4,514	53	39
Muslims	3,678	49	43
Christians	5,920	81	27
Other Minorities	5,427	54	34
All India	4,485	54	39

An analysis based on Table 1 reveals that the per capita income and the literacy rate of Muslim households surveyed were lower as compared to other minorities and Hindus and these were also lower than the all India averages, respectively. So far as the percentage of population living below the poverty line is concerned, 43% of Muslim households belonged to this category and this is higher as compared to other minorities and Hindus and Hindus are just at par with all India average.

Further, an analysis of household income based on Table 2 reveals that 44.1% of the household income of Muslims come from agriculture and allied activities, 14.7% from salaried employment, 9.9% from petty trade and small business, 8.3% from artisan and industrial work, 7.7% from agricultural wages and 7.4% from non-agricultural wages and the residual income from other sources. In the case of other minorities and Hindus, the percentage of household income which comes from agriculture is higher than the Muslims.

TABLE 2

Percentage Distribution of Household Income by Source Across Religious Groups

Religious Groups	*Percentage Distribution of Total Household Income*										*All Sources*
	Agr+Alld Activity	*Artisan/ Ind.Work*	*Petty Trd.*	*Orgn. Trd.*	*Sala Empl*	*Quali Prof.*	*Rent/ Int*	*Agri Wage*	*Non-Agri sources*	*Other*	
Hindu	56.1	4.3	4.6	1.8	16.4	0.5	0.6	8.0	6.2	1.5	100.0
Muslims	44.1	8.3	9.9	2.9	14.7	0.8	0.5	7.7	7.4	3.8	100.0
Christians	46.3	2.9	4.1	1.9	23.5	0.4	0.5	9.4	7.8	3.1	100.0
Other Minorities	60.3	3.1	3.7	0.6	17.6	0.8	1.9	5.2	5.0	1.7	100.0
All India	55.0	4.5	5.0	1.9	16.5	0.5 .	0.7	7.9	6.3	1.7	100.0

TABLE 3

Amenities Available in Household by Religious Groups

Religious Groups	*Percentage of Household Owing*				
	Kutcha House	*Separate Kitchen*	*Electric Connection*	*Protected Water*	*Toilet*
Hindus	55.2	41.5	43.2	71.1	13.2
Muslims	65.9	44.7	30.0	78.1	26.7
Christians	34.2	68.8	59.9	64.7	50.3
Other Minorities	43.0	42.7	60.5	83.2	14.1
All India	**55.4**	**42.4**	**42.9**	**72.0**	**15.3**

Interestingly, Table 3 reveals that almost 60% of Muslim households were living in Kutcha house and this percentage is higher as compared to other minorities and Hindus. Only 30% of Muslim households reported electric connection and only 19% reported piped water.

TABLE 4

Literacy Rates (Percentage) and Gender Disparity by Religious Groups

Religious Groups	*Literacy Rates (Aged 7 & above)*			*F/M*
	Persons	*Male*	*Female*	
Hindus	55.3	65.9	39.2	0.60
Muslims	49.4	59.5	38.0	0.64
Christians	80.8	85.0	76.5	0.90
Other Minorities	53.8	62.9	43.8	0.70
All India	**53.5**	**65.6**	**40.1**	**0.61**

Table 4 reveals lower literacy rate among Muslim males as well as females as compared to other minorities and Hindus. Similarly, gender disparity, in this respect, is also higher in case of Muslims as compared to other minorities.

As a matter of fact, Table 5 reveals that crude birth rate (CBR) and total fertility rate (TFR) are also higher as compared to other minorities and Hindus. Crude birth rate (CDR) is, more less, the same in the case of Muslims and other communities except Christians.

TABLE 5

Fertility and Mortality Rates by Religious Groups

Religious Groups	*CBR/000*	*TFR(15-49)*	*CDR/000*
Hindus	32	4.2	11
Muslims	39	5.8	10
Christians	20	2.1	8
Other Minorities	28	3.9	11
All India	**32**	**4.3**	**11**

India is a country of diversities in the social and economic spheres. Although, there are wide variations in rural and urban areas, but within rural areas, notable differentials exist not only at state level but also at district and community levels despite 50 years of our development experience.

Politicization of Relative Growth Issues

We have adopted parliamentary form of democracy and we can overthrow the coalition formations through elections. Therefore, political mobilization along religion and cost lines is not anything new in India, but Northern India has become the epitome of sectarian politics. By 1990, Indian politics has become *triangular*. Between 1950 and 1990, the principal battle-lines of politics were *bipolar*. The Congress was the party of Government and all other parties were opposed to it. Between 1950 and 1997, a triangular contest developed between the left, the Hindus nationalists, and the Congress party. The left and the lower caste Janata Dal wanted to organize the lower Hindus castes against the upper castes, whereas Hindu nationalists were trying to build a united Hindu community against the Muslims, seeking to over-ride and displace castes as an issue in political mobilization. The triumph of one implied the eclipse of other. The Congress party, a foe in the past but declining ideologically, was no longer the principal enemy of the Janata Party. Thus, Hindu-Muslim relations and caste animosities became the prime determinant of political coalitions.

To cater better to minorities, the Government of India launched a 15- point programme which can be broadly classified into three categories: security of life and property, reservation in government services and socio-economic development. Though, the government reports claim that lot of progress has been made in these areas, but the ground realities speak otherwise.

Areas of Policy Concerns

Following are the critical areas which require immediate attention from the policy makers and others concerned with the prevailing conflict between *good economics* and *good politics* because earlier both of them used to walk side-by-side, but now both of them are running into the opposite direction:

- Politicization of the anatomy of Ayodhya case;
- Politicization of religious trusts and economic trust worthiness;
- Inter-state disparities and regionalization and communization of Indian politics;
- Political economy of unbalanced regional development;
- Regional and local analysis of vote-bank politics and development issues;

- A point-by-point impact analysis of the 15-point programme for minorities;
- Political economy of communal riots;
- Divergence between political means and economic ends;
- Balkanization of Indian political economy into Hindu and Muslim political economy;
- Study of Lok Sabha Debates on minority related issues during the last 50 years of Indian democracy;
- All-inclusive multi-pronged strategy of democratic development;
- Alternative formula for re-alignment between religious polity and economy;
- Coalition politics and coalition economic policy; and
- A contextual review of *political economy*, as a discipline, from *police state-to welfare state-to state-led development*.

10

THE INDIAN MUSLIMS: THEIR SOCIO-ECONOMIC STATUS

—Abhinav Sharma

There exist 110 million Muslims in India—which, with the exception of Indonesia—is the largest population of Muslims in a single country in the world. Muslim communities in India are geographically scattered, culturally diverse and economically disparate. Their economic and social progress is very crucial for the development of the country. No country can boast of development if its sizeable minority lags behind and if its large population remains illiterate and poor.

Although the constitution of India provides for certain provisions for the promotion of rights of minorities yet the government machinery has been lackadaisical in responding to individual and collective efforts to redress the inequities and imbalances in private and public sectors. It was in 1983 that government of India realised the significance of the minorities by setting up Gopal Singh Committee to prepare a status report. The committee declared the Muslims as one of the most backward minority communities of the country. According to it about half the Muslims population lived below the poverty line. The report also furnished information on widespread illiteracy and a higher drop-out rate at the elementary stage of education.

In 1983, the Muslims were not only grossly under-represented in public services, but were predominant in the 'Self-employed' category. The report of the sub-group on minorities (1996) constituted by the Planning Commission illustrates that there are no signs of significant improvement. Whether it is the police or the railways, the state or the all-India services, the relatively fewer urban Muslim work for a regular wage or salary, and their representation in the 'casual labour category' is higher than of other communities. Abusaleh Shariff's seminal study reveals that, in urban India, 53.4 per cent of Muslims are self-employed as against the figure of 36 per cent amongst Hindus. In rural areas the annual household income for Muslims as a social group is below the all-India average, as well as below that of Christians.

Not a single Muslims figured among the 50 industrial houses up till 1985. Muslim industrialists owned only 4 units in a group of 2,832 industrial enterprises, each with sales of Rs. 50 million and above. In the smaller industrial sector, they owned about 14,000 units of a total of 600,000 of which 2,000 belonged to the 'small' category with a limited capital outlay. Apart from this the skills of Muslims are by and large traditional and they happen to be primary producers and totally lack marketing skills. In today's globalised world people with traditional skills cannot survive longer, much less prosper. But where there is lack of even primary literacy there is no question of upgradation of skills. The educational backwardness reflects economic backwardness and economic backwardness perpetrates educational backwardness. Thus it has become a vicious circle. The literacy level is on an average 10 per cent less than the concedes that the Muslims, their women and girls included, remain educationally backward and their traditional institutions like 'madarsas' are yet to adopt the modern syllabus to get integrated into the mainstream education.

Today we are giving much emphasis on human rights and human development. This will be a farce if the predominant Muslims minority community is left far behind from the benefits provided by the welfare state.

11

SCOPE FOR MODERNISATION OF MADARSAS IN INDIA

—Noor Mohammad

> 'Allah will raise up those who have knowledge'
>
> *(Surah 58 Ayah 11)*

> Allah's Messenger (peace be upon him) said, "A father gives his son nothing better than a good education." (Narrated by Amr ibn Sa'id ibn al-'As in *Al Tirmidhi*)

The very first message of Islam was on education. The first verse of *Quran* (Surah Al-Alaq also known as Surah-I-Iqra) gives the message to 'read'. The message was for all human beings and for all men and women.

In addition, *Quran* is replete with verses inviting people to use their intellect, to ponder, to think and to know. Islam recognizes that the goal of human life is to discover the truth and equates this discovery with worshipping god in his oneness. The *Hadith* literature is also full of references to the importance of knowledge. Such sayings of the prophet as "Seek knowledge even in China"(It is notable that China, at that time, was not famous for Islamic learning but for new inventions like paper, potteries etc.),"Seek knowledge from the cradle to the grave", and "verily the men of knowledge are the inheritors of the prophets", have echoed throughout the history of Islam and incited Muslims to seek knowledge wherever it might be found. That is why every traditional Islamic city possessed public and private libraries and some cities like Cordoba in Spain and Baghdad boasted of libraries with over 400,000 books. Such cities also had bookstores, some of which sold a large number of titles. That is also why the scholars have always been held in the highest esteem in Islamic society. This paper aims at finding out scope for modernization of madarsa system of education and attempts a model for the same.

The Attitude of Islam Towards Knowledge

Importance of education in Islam is reflected in the famous Hudaibia treaty signed after the battle of Badr. In this treaty prisoners of war (the Meccans) who were learned, were given the option to educate Muslims of Medina for their release. It is to be noted that the Meccans at that time were not known for Quranic teachings. However, the focus in the initial years was limited to Quranic teachings, which later covered other fields of knowledge. Early Ummayyed period seems to mark the beginning of formal elementary education that developed in the newly conquered land of Iraq, Syria and Persia. Under the Abbasids, when Muslims came under influence of Greek literature and philosophy and became acquainted with Indian sciences namely medicine, mathematics and astronomy, the formal education got a big boost. Scholars like al-Ghazzali on one hand emphasized that closeness to Allah can be attained only through knowledge (of religion) and on the other hand underlined the importance of sciences useful for civil and social purposes. Study of medicine, arithmetic, horticulture, weaving etc., were also considered essential for society and hence were to be included in education.

MADARSA—ITS JOURNEY THROUGH HISTORY

There were no formal educational institutions during the early days of Islam. The first major attempt to establish such institutions seems to have been made during the 4th century Hijri when Nishapur Madarsa was established in Khurasan. Caliph, Al-Mamun, a great patron of learning, founded madarsa at Baghdad, Al-Kufa and Bokhara. To establish a madarsa or maktab has always been treated as a pious objective in Islam and hence these institutions have been promoted initially by the rulers and later even by the community and its well-wishers.

The objective of these institution has been largely to impart religious education and to spread the teachings of Holy *Quran*. Subsequently, services and humanities were included in the syllabi. Muslim scholars translated Greek and Indian knowledge and worked to develop it further. To discover secrets of nature was a pious purpose and scholars like Ibn-I-Khaldun, Ibn Asir, Imam-al-Ghazzali, Imam Fakhr-ud-din Razi, Abu Ali Ibn Sena, Nizam-ul-Mulk Tusi, Umar Khayyam, Sadi and Hafiz among many others made invaluable contributions to human knowledge.

In ancient India, education was imparted through the Gurukulas and Sanskrit Pathshalas. These institutions were benefiting largely the upper castes in the cast based Indian society. These institutions trained rulers, administrators and also imparted religious knowledge largely confined to Brahmins who helped the society in observing the religious rituals. During the Sultanates and Mughal periods, the official language changed to Persian and non-Muslims who occupied positions in government were also attracted to madarsas to learn Persian so as to qualify for the state jobs. Raja Todar Mal is one such star that still shines and his contribution are still remembered. For a fairly long time, these madarsas served the society – Hindus and Muslims and imparted education to them. The *Mahabharata*, *Ramayana*, *Atharvaveda* etc. were translated into Persian and this fusion of knowledge from both these great civilizations contributed, a great deal, to the growth of a composite culture.

The Sultanate period witnessed the evolution of languages, which later were known as Urdu and Hindi. The sultanate rulers, with large areas under their control, had to communicate with the common masses that spoke different languages. If it was Braj near Agra, it was Avadhi in Avadh and Bhojpuri in the Eastern Uttar Pradesh. Kumaon spoke Kumayuni and Garhwal communicated in Garhwali. These were regional languages confined to small regions and were full-fledged languages in their own right. A language was evolved from these and other regional languages with a view to increase communication between the ruler and the ruled. Surprisingly, this appears to be the only effort to make the language of the rulers and the common masses the same. This language often referred to as 'Hindustani' was written in Deonagri in some part of the land, while in other places it was written in Persian script, of which today's Sanskrit's Hindi and Persianised Urdu are the present incarnations.

With the change of medium of Urdu, madarsas contributed to produce clerks for local government offices and courts till India's independence when Hindi was made the national language and madarsa's relevance in this regard was lost. As a result madarsas largely confined themselves to religious education, classical Arabic and classical Persian in the years that followed. Of late there have been some moves to modernize the madarsa education by bringing in English, Hindi, Humanities, Mathematics and Sciences in the curricula, though the effort remains much below the desired level.

A concerted effort is needed to make these institutions more viable in terms of their contribution to the society in general and to the Muslim community in particular. A three-point programme to fulfil these objectives is being suggested below.

3–POINT PROGRAMME FOR EDUCATIONAL DEVELOPMENT

POINT–1 - 'EDUCATION FOR ALL' (EFA) FOR MINORITIES

Universalisation of Elementary Education (UEE) has remained an elusive dream even after 55 years of Independence. The situation is even more dismal amongst educationally backward communities like Muslims. Below are some suggestions to achieve the goal of EFA amongst Muslims.

TRADITIONAL EDUCATIONAL INSTITUTIONS

Maktab

There are about 30,000 Maktabs in Uttar Pradesh alone where teaching is limited to reading of the Holy *Quran* and a little bit of Urdu. These Maktabs can be converted into Non-Formal Education (NFE) centers by providing another local teacher to teach Hindi, Elementary Maths and English. After the NFE a child can join the regular stream through admission to the 6th standard in government schools.

Bangladesh experiment to modernize Maktab Education can be replicated with the help of UNICEF who have collaborated the experiment in Bangladesh. This step amounts to opening 30,000 primary schools for Muslims overnight in U.P. alone.

Madarsa

There are about 2000 Arabic/Persian Madarsas in Uttar Pradesh alone where students spends up to 16 years on studies. The following table shows the exams passed and the years spent by a student in Madarsas:

Name of examination	*Years spent*
Tahtania	5 Years
Fauqania	8 Years (3 years after Tahtania)
Munshi/Maulavi	10 Years (2 years after Fauqania)
Alim	12 Years (2 years after Munshi /Maulavi)
Kamil	14 Years (2 years after Alim)
Fazil	16 Years (2 years after Kamil)

In Uttar Pradesh, these institutions are presently teaching only Muslim Theology. There have been experiments in Bihar and West Bengal to modernize these institutions so as include modern education in Madarsas together with the study of religion. The experiment can be replicated in other states as well and in fact an improved version can be adopted so as to ensure that the learning levels of the students is commensurate with the number of years he spends in modern institutions. For instance an Alim should be in a position to compete High Secondary School pass outs. Such a step will mean opening of about 2000 Intermediate colleges in U.P. and some of these may be converted into even Degree/Post Graduate Colleges.

Founding such an efforts up to 8th standard (Fauqania) can come partly from Modernization of Madarsa scheme under the New Education Policy, 1986. Funds of Maulana Azad Educational Trust can be utilized for these modernization efforts. Some funds can also be raised from World Bank, UNICEF and even Islamic Development Bank. Madarsa adoption scheme (on the patterns adopted for schools in Madhya Pradesh) can be encouraged for quicker result.

It is also important that the Certificate/Degrees awarded by these institutions are recognized. Government of U.P. has issued orders recognizing Munshi/Maulvi as High School, and Alim equivalent to Intermediate levels. Department of Higher Education in U.P. has addressed letters to the state universities to recognize Kamil and Fazil degrees as Graduate and Post Graduate degrees respectively. But such recognition is meaningless if the learning levels, in the madarsas giving out such certificates/ degrees, does not improve and come near the learning levels in the Universities.

Implementation of the Plan of Action, 1992

Comprehensive provision have been made for education of educationally backward communities in the Plan of Action –1992, a document issued by the Ministry of Human Resource Development (HRD). The implementation of this plan of action should be effectively monitored and demand for adequate funds must be made from the central government and provision of funds may also be made by the State to provide the missing links.

Technical/Medical Education

Muslims are far behind in Technical/Medical Education. The reasons are two folds. One, it is too costly to afford. Two, admission itself is difficult – Muslim boys and girls are unable to compete, as their home environment does not permit them to prepare for such a competition.

Educational finance, institutional or non-institutional,

on easy terms can be helpful to finance their education and remedial coaching can help the Muslim boys and girls in Entrance Examination for these courses. Though there has been a UGC coaching scheme, nothing noticeable has happened.

The best solution is to allow the Muslim organizations to open Technical /Medical College and grant State Government's no objection and recognition by the respective Councils (like AICTE for Engineering) in the Central Government liberally. But even this will not solve the problem as admission to these institutions have to be done only on merit or on payment of heavy donations. Therefore, the only alternative is to grant them the status of minority institutions as a result of which, 50% Muslim boys /girls can be admitted in these institutions.

Vocational Training

Muslims are good artisans. They are good mechanics. They are marvelous tailors. Only problem is that their skills are transferred from generation to generation thereby leaving little room for modernization. It is important to upgrade skills of the artisans already engaged as training the unemployed youth both in rural and urban areas so that new artisans enter the vocation. Monitoring of the training schemes should be done in terms of the number of persons actively employed after training. There should be vocation specific schemes to transform these sectors. Some specific schemes are as follows:

1. Short duration training has to be organized with a view to help the prospective artisan to take up a vocation. Training, funding etc. should form a comprehensive package.

   (a) There have been almost unlimited funds for

training in the IDRP. The scheme known as Training of Rural Youth for Self Employment (TRYSEM) can be implemented vigorously and monitored effectively to enable unemployed youth in Rural Areas to take up self-employment.

(b) NRY has been started for Urban Areas but the pattern is more or less the same as TRYSEM. This programme can also be implemented effectively with a view to promote self-employment.

2. A large number of Muslims are engaged in services like driving, motor mechanics, tailoring etc. There are no institutions, which provide certificates/ diplomas in these fields. A scheme for training the existing artisans in upgrading their skills and for training the unemployed youth for new jobs is very much needed. There is a great potential in this. For instance a tailor presently earning meagre income can become a fashion designer in case he is educated enough and a comprehensive training for 6 months to 1 year is provided to enable him to take up such a job in tailoring shops or on self-employment basis.

POINT-2 - INCOME GENERATION SCHEMES

A good law and order situation is a precursor for any economic development. Therefore, preventive steps to ensure that riots do not take place should become an integral part of the District's Riot Plans. In addition, the following issues need immediate consideration:

1. Schemes of the Government of India for handloom weavers are implemented more on paper. Better implementation will help the handloom sector.
2. There should be flow of bank credit in proportion of their population.

3. Urban Co-operative Development Banks sponsored by minorities must be permitted liberally to ensure easy access to credit.
4. The benefit flowing from the government schemes should go to member of the minorities in proportion of their population.
5. Minority Commission of the state may be authorized to look into the grievances faced by the members of the minority communities while setting up an industry.
6. Vocation specific diseases like eye diseases amongst bangle and chikan workers, lung diseases amongst leather and lock industry workers etc., have to be tackled in a planned manner. Most of the artisans are from minority communities and are located in compact geographical areas and therefore area specific schemes can be formulated for this purpose.
7. There should be some efforts to modernize weaver's looms and to upgrade quality of product design. Similarly, other handicraft artisans should be provided better tools to work, so that artisan's income can be increased and more persons can be employed in this sector.

In brief, efforts should be made to ensure that the Muslims are not at a disadvantage (due to illiteracy or ignorance) while taking recourse to the government schemes.

POINT–3 – UTILIZATION OF THE INSTITUTION OF WAQFS FOR EDUCATIONAL DEVELOPMENT

The safety and management of Waqfs has been the main issues raised by the community leaders from time to time. The development of Waqfs and development through Waqfs have not received the attention they deserve. A lot remains to be done in these important areas.

Safety of Waqf Properties

Due to increase in urban limits, graveyards (a king of Waqf) have come in the populated areas and value of the land has increased. This has resulted in large-scale encroachments on these lands. Waqf lands are under threat from land grabbers and some times governments have occupied prime lands, and such encroached lands are entered in records as government nazul lands. In addition, land in rural areas and that situated in the vicinity of Mazars is occupied by influential people with connivance of the local revenue officials. Other Waqf properties are also badly managed and either the mutawallia or other influential people are using these properties unauthorized for their personal gains.

A comprehensive plan can be formulated to give government support in implementing the provisions of the Waqf Acts so as to save these properties from wrong use. Due to apathy of government officials, Waqf Acts provisions become ineffective and security of these properties is under threat.

Waqf properties are under the Rent Control Act and therefore, one can find shops owned by Waqfs skill at Rs. 5/- per month of rent. In U.P. these properties have been exempted from the Rent Control Regime but situation on the ground has remained more or less unchanged. Some efforts are needed to ensure that reasonable returns are guaranteed to these Waqfs.

In addition to safety of Waqfs, these properties can be developed. Some states have created Waqf Development Corporations. Waqfs can be helped to develop commercial complexes in the areas where land costs have gone very high and utilize the income from such complexes in running Engineering/Medical College and other Technical Institutions for higher education. Such institutions can be built on the Waqf lands that lie in the periphery of the towns where the value of the land is low. Increased income of Waqfs can also be utilized to fulfill the Waqf objectives and to finance other activities for the benefit of the society at large.

Development Through Waqf Institution

Waqfs like many other institutions established by Muslims can be utilized as Non-Government Organizations (NGOs) for ensuring participation of minority communities in the government sponsored schemes. Waqfs are organization registered under the Waqf Acts and are like other NGOs, which are registered either under the Societies Act or the Trust Act. Schemes run by the government through the NGOs, facilities given to NGOs for schemes on literacy, primary education, women and child development, family welfare etc. should be entrusted to Waqf institution that want to take up these activities as NGOs.

Conclusion

The common understanding that Madarsas/Maktabs are meant to impart only religious education is flawed. On the other hand, these institutions should be treated as any educational institution capable of imparting complete education to people. Misunderstanding about these institutions that have been allowed to develop of late have to be cleared, the genuine problems facing the Madarsas/ Maktabs have to be attended to and services of these institutions have to be taken to impart education to the people. When grazing grounds can be promoted to start

Charwaha Schools, why madarsas cannot be encouraged to contribute their bit.

A sizeable number of Arabic/Persian madarsas can be upgraded to High School, Intermediate levels incorporating modern curricula. And quite a few of them can be upgraded to impart higher education as well. At least a few of them can be converted into Engineering, Medical and Management schools. These institutions can also be given the responsibility of coordinating government efforts/ facilities with the community leaders in their areas. An apex organization, consisting of well meaning individuals, retired Government servants etc. willing to do social service, at the All India level with its state units may be set up to coordinate and provide consultancy services to different local efforts to utilize these existing madarsas, Waqf bodies and charitable trusts as agents for educational and economic development of the community. One learns from one's failures and it is high time that the Muslim community learnt from the past without losing time any further.

12

EMPOWERMENT OF MUSLIM WOMEN IN INDIA: THE EMERGING PERSPECTIVE

—*Awadhesh Kumar Singh*

The well being of people is unquestionably the ultimate object of all development efforts of a country and the basic quest of human endeavour is always to seek a better quality of life. The quality of life of citizens of a nation can be effectively improved only by raising the standards of living of the people on the street and in rural areas. Social empowerment in general and women empowerment in particular is very fundamental in achieving this goal. This institution of democracy provides a strong foundation for harmonizing social and economic objectives. Thus within the broad democratic framework there are great opportunities for synergying women and economic growth programmes to deliver better quality of life in the shortest possible span of time. In India, the plight of Muslim women is not better than that of women belonging to other social groups. Despite the honour and reverence accorded to women as deities in religion and mythology and tribute paid to them as personified in historical monuments, the ground realities have a very different tale to tell. In a patriarchal society like India, there exists the unfounded belief that only man is the bread-earner of the family, consequently, the male child gets the best of the limited facilities and resources within the family. The girl child runs the risk of being aborted through the misuse of modern technique of amniocenteses. She is deprived of quality school education because she has to take care of siblings at home and since she is to be married off soon, investing in her education is considered wasteful and hence a liability. More than half a century of Independence, the efforts of striving for a better status for women have not yielded satisfactory results in India. Indian women are at the crossroads of their denting. There is a great upsurge in consciousness about their rights among all sections and class of society in all regions of the country. There has been a tremendous increase in the developmental activities for woman since the 1980s with a great leap forward in the 1990s. Interestingly, Muslim women in India have been playing a subordinate role though Constitution of India establishes a secular state and eliminates discrimination ground of race, religion, sex etc. Muslim women continue to be victims of traditional social structure of the community. It is evident from the fact that educational development among the Muslim women is very poor and due to this their economic participation is quite low. Muslim women are also not enjoying the equal status in the society due to cultural and religious traditions, norms and values of the society. The provision of divorce, polygamy, Mehr has placed women in a lower status.

Due to the impact of modernization, westernization, globalisation, democracy, socio-economic changes, legal enactment pertaining to Muslim women, society is advancing towards gender just and equates systems, giving the way to empowerment and advancement of Muslim women in India. Against this perspective, present paper attempts to review the plight of Muslim Women in India and to analyse the emerging perspectives of their development. The paper also attempts to present a package of policy recommendations for their empowerment.

Status of Muslim Women

The status of Muslim women in India is not better than that of other women. Muslim woman in India is influenced by the Islamic injunctions and also the impact of the Hindu culture and traditions because mostly Indian Muslims are converts from Hinduism. If we want to know the changing status and role of Muslim women in India, it would be better to give a brief account from traditional period to contemporary period. It is interesting because India was invaded by different rulers in the past. These invasions had definitely influenced the Indian women.

Mostly, women studies in India have concentrated on the Hindu women, so there is a paucity of research materials on Muslims women. Available literature indicates that Indian women, who were free, enjoyed a equal status with their men folk during this ancient period. Neither seclusion nor early marriage was prevalent during this period, women were allowed to have their say in selection of males and a widow was allowed to re-marry. They also had share in the parental property. As a whole we find that in this period the position of women was high within the framework of a patriarchal society.

After the Independence the significant changes that have taken place for the betterment of women did not affect the lot of the Muslims in the country. This had been mainly because the Muslim community as such was, at the time of political power, more involved and concerned over the partition of the country on the basis of religion (Bhatty, 1976).

The partition of India in 1947 did not solve the Muslim problem, since it left 45 million Muslims in India. The migration of 6 million Muslims, one-third of total Indian Muslim population, affected the tradition Muslim strongholds of Delhi, Western Uttar Pradesh, south Bihar, Kolkata, Mumbai, Bhopal, Ahmedabad, Hyderabad and Chennai. The urban migrants were many the young, educated intelligentsia primarily from the professions (Imam, 1975). Migration from the rural areas was marginal (10 per cent), with the exception of east Punjab, and therefore, its impact on urban migration created serious disequilibrium in the social, political and economic status of the community. For the 70 million Muslims in India today, 1947 was the watershed, and the period, which followed, was one of the painful adjustment. The interactive bloodshed that followed polarized communities and inflicted sears which have still to heal (Lateef, 1983).

There also developed a polarity within the Muslims community. With the thinning of the educated intelligentsia from the urban areas there was a preponderance of Muslims from the lower socio-economic strata. Continuing commercial tensions since independence have created urban Muslim ghettoes .The reasons for these tensions lie as much in historical factors as in the present struggle for survival, where Muslims compete with the lower strata of other communities. We therefore have parallel class stratification hierarchies in different communities with overlapping class interests among their elites who have a stake in maintaining the stability of the existing social order (Enloce, 1973).

However, burgeoning expectation, a phenomenon of mass communication and urbanization, make the lower strata group within a community impatient for change even as they challenge the inequalities of the existing social hierarchy. These also increase the rivalry between similar strata groups of other communities rather than uniting them for a joint effort at social change. Once confined to the ghetto, it becomes difficult for individuals to break away, with poverty, isolation and conservation reinforcing each other. This has very seriously affected the Muslim women who, already hampered by purdah, lack of education and general seclusion, becomes plagued with an additional sense of insecurity vis-à-vis the other communities. Her status is derived from the family, i.e., the male head, so she tends to suffer not the disabilities attached to the female status, but also to the family's status in the class hierarchy (Parkin, 1971).

The gap between Muslims in the ghettoes and the tiny Muslim elite is enormous. Successful Muslims men and women are already participants in the modernization process. The Muslims women in this privileged position, is confident that her husband will not take another wife (the 1961 census revealed that the incidence of bigamous marriage among Muslims are lower than among Hindus, presumable because in this reference group such marriages are not no longer acceptable .a small incidence of unilateral divorce in place of polygamy is however, reported).

The above analysis simply demonstrates that the plight of Muslim women in India is not better than of women belonging to other social communities. Moreover, majority of the Muslims women are illiterate, low educated and living in the absolute poverty. Importantly, most of the Muslim women are confined to four walls of the house and have been assigned the domestic work, caring and nourishing of children, performing household activities etc. Only a small segment of the Muslim women are engaged in economic activities for substantial income contribution to families. Moreover, the role conflict among such women has been observed to be high since they are facing the problems of the official tasks and orthodox family attitude. Through, education and other factors have significantly changed the environment and Muslims women have started enjoying the liberal and democratic advantages and benefits.

Moreover, a significant number of Muslims women have started peeping out their heads to participate in the development process due to the changed socio-economic environment. Importantly, the young generation is demanding more liberty and breaking the orthodox norms of Muslims community. This demands the concerted efforts on the part of the government and non-government for empowerment of women and making them crucial counterparts of the society for social advancement.

EDUCATIONAL DEVELOPMENT

The scenario of education among Indian Muslims is depressing and disheartening .The causes are not far to seek globally; the last centuries have witnessed the phenomenon of the Muslim, withdrawal and stagnation. Moreover, the standard of teaching in Muslim schools and colleges, with some exception is indifferent.

There result are often poor and sometimes it is the Non-Muslim students on roll who prevent the average from going down further. Again, Muslim parents by and large, adopt an attitude of non-challenge towards their children's education. Those parents who are educated and their number is not large, have little time or inclination for helping their children with the home work. This results in Muslim students being deprived of the environment and guidance so necessary in the earlier stages of education.

The NFHS survey also reveals that educational levels among Muslim women are highly lower as compared to women belonging to other social groups. Illiteracy rate was recorded highest i.e. 60.5 per cent among Muslim women while it was recorded as low as 6.8 per cent among Jain women. Dr. O.P. Gupta made a comparative study of rural schools of four districts in Uttar Pradesh with reference to school culture, Text books and facilities for teaching Urdu and through Urdu medium for his doctoral dissertation. The data pertaining to the results of annual examination conducted in March-April, 1976. The analysis of data demonstrates that in all four districts – Moradabad, Saharanpur, Etah and Etawah, the enrolment of Muslim students was not proportionate. It shows that Muslims are lagging behind Hindus in the terms of the enrolment proportion. Again the Academic achievement as seen through results, of both Hindus and Muslims for class VI to X, indicate that Muslims have not done as good as the Hindus. The enrolment proportions in the four districts indicate the trend of discriminations that as the proportion of Muslims decreases, the level of discrimination also decreases. It can be interpreted that the discrimination tends to become imperceptible with the decreasing population. Moreover, differences in the achievement of Hindu-Muslim students are significant. These differences are more within the schools than between the schools. Factors like teacher, text books, facilities, economic background of the two communities being the same, only these school factors, which can have differential effect of two sets of students, can account for differences in educational achievement of the students of two communities. The study reveals that school culture, text–book, absence of facilities for teaching Urdu are the only factors that tends to have differential effect on the two communities. The nationalized text books of Hindi, Sanskrit and social studies as used for classes VI to X in the school of U.P. contains objectionable materials from Muslims points of view, not a single school out of 111 has Urdu as a medium of instructions and both students and parents object to this aspect of schooling. Moreover, only to schools out of 111 provide facilities for the study of the Urdu as a subject from class VI to VII. Three out of the aforesaid 10 schools have provisions for study of Urdu up to class X. Schools culture is full of Hindu religion practices and is visible in the dramas that are enacted in the schools and prayers and pujas that are organized.

TABLE 1

Educational Levels among Social Groups

Level of Education	*Women belonging to different social groups*						
	Hindu	*Muslim*	*Christian*	*Sikh*	*Jain*	*Buddhist*	*Other*
Illiterate	59.3	60.5	32.9	38.9	6.8	44.7	70.3
Literate Primary School complete	5.4	9.5	7.3	3.0	2.5	10.8	6.2
Primary School Complete	13.0	14.8	15.4	18.1	22.6	14.6	8.5
Middle School Complete	8.3	6.1	13.1	9.8	14.3	13.2	8.8
High School Complete	7.2	5.6	14.6	16.4	23.4	8.9	4.0
Higher Secondary Complete and above	6.8	3.5	16.7	13.8	30.4	7.9	2.1
Total	100.00	100.00	100.00	100.00	100.00	100.00	100.00

Source: National Family Health Survey, 1998-99., IIPS, Mumbai.

The NFHS Survey also reveals that educational levels among Muslim women are highly lower as compared to women belonging to other social groups. Illiteracy rate was recorded highest i.e. 60.5 per cent among Muslim women while it was recorded as low as 6.8 per cent among Jain women. Moreover higher education was reported lowest among Muslim women as compared to women belonging to other social groups (Table 1).

Data available from report on minorities of high power panel on minorities, SCs, STs, and other weaker sections, in Uttar Pradesh during1980-1981, participation of Muslims in the elementary education shows a dismal picture. Muslim population comprises 17.32 per cent in total population of country while enrollment in class I to VIII of Muslims was reported just 12.39 per cent and less comparatively as low as 8.46 per cent in U.P. the enrollment of Muslim children in class I to VIII was reported as low as 0.69 per cent in Gorakhpur, 1.38 per cent in Jaunpur and 2.02 per cent in Raibareilly, though enrollment of Muslims was found some what satisfactory in Moradabad followed by Rampur and Saharanpur, the dropout at primary level (class I to V) among all communities was reported 64.61 per cent at national level and much higher at state level. Moreover dropout at primary level among Muslims was reported slightly higher i.e. 64.82 per cent at national level and much more at state level. As compared dropout rate among all communities with Muslim community was recorded higher in Nainital, Rampur and Saharanpur while at state level it was reported 90.54 per cent as against other religious categories.

Although, religion and caste have an impact on many types of social behaviour in India, such as opting for a secular education normally imparted by public institution. ST s and SC s recorded a literacy level of about 40 per cent. Muslims on the contrary have literacy level of about 50 per cent. While female literacy is significantly low for all social groups. (India Human Development Report, 1999). Data also show that high literacy levels have been found more pronouncing among Christians and Hindus while Muslims are lagging behind in terms of achieving educational level of matriculation and above.

FAMILY PLANNING

Muslims have the highest fertility; followed by Hindus and other religions have the lowest fertility. Muslim's fertility is higher than Hindu fertility (equivalent to half a child, on the average).

Scheduled tribes have the highest fertility of any groups followed by scheduled castes. Importantly, total fertility rate among Muslims was recorded 3.59 children per woman as per report of national family health service, 1998-1999 (Table 2).

TABLE 2

Fertility Rate among Social Groups

Particular	*Women belonging to different social groups*						
	Hindu	*Muslim*	*Christian*	*Sikh*	*Jain*	*Buddhist*	*Other*
Total Fertility Rate(15-49 year)	2.78	3.59	2.44	2.26	1.90	2.13	2.33
Percentage of currently pregnant women	5.5	6.9	4.3	4.8	—	3.7	5.0
Mean number of children ever born to ever married women age 40-49 years	4.34	5.72	3.47	3.59	3.32	4.05	4.33

Source: National Family Health Survey, 1998-99.

Information about knowledge of family planning and the use of contraceptive methods is of practical use of policy makers and programme administrators for formulating policies and strategies. This part of paper begins with an appraisal of the knowledge of contraceptive method and knowledge of sources of supply of modern contraceptive method before moving on to a consideration of current and past practice of family planning. Special attention is focused on non-use, reason for discontinuation, and intention to use family planning in the future.

Knowledge about sterilization is widespread in Uttar Pradesh. This is also true for female sterilization. In comparison, the three officially sponsored spacing methods, namely IUD, pill and condom, are much less familiar. The best known among the spacing methods are condoms and pills. Injections are the least known. Moreover, traditional methods of contraception are generally less well known than modern methods, periodic abstinence being better known than the withdrawal method, again differentials in the level of knowledge of modern contraceptive method and sources of methods among currently married women, are shown according to background characteristics. Interestingly, contraceptive sources are relatively less well known among Muslims and women from scheduled tribes (NFHS, 1998-1999).

Current use of contraception in U.P. was low, with only 20 per cent of currently married women practicing family planning; 19 per cent using modern methods and another 1 per cent were using traditional methods (NFHS, 1992-1993). Most of the currently married women who had ever used contraception were currently using a method. Religious differential in the prevalence of contraception are also quite substantial. The prevalence rate was lowest. NFHS-2, 1998-1999 also reveals that current use of family planning among Muslim women is comparatively low (Table 3).

TABLE 3

Current Use of Family Planning among Social Groups

Particular	*Women belonging to different social groups*						
	Hindu	*Muslim*	*Christian*	*Sikh*	*Jain*	*Buddhist*	*Other*
Any method	49.2	37.0	52.4	65.2	65.1	64.7	68.6
Any Modern Method	44.3	30.2	44.9	54.7	58.1	63.9	35.2
Pill	1.8	4.1	1.2	3.7	0.2	2.5	2.8
IUD	1.5	1.5	2.3	7.4	4.3	1.4	3.9
Condom	2.7	4.2	2.8	11.8	10.0	2.5	1.5
Female Sterilization	36.2	19.6	36.5	30.2	42.3	52.5	26.1
Male Sterilization	2.1	0.8	2.1	1.6	1.4	5.0	1.0
Any Traditional Method	4.7	6.4	7.1	10.1	6.4	0.8	9.1
Rhythm /Safe Period	2.9	3.6	4.9	4.6	4.6	0.4	4.9
Withdrawal	1.8	2.8	2.3	5.5	1.8	0.4	4.3
Other Method	0.3	0.4	0.4	0.4	0.6	0.0	4.2
Not Using Any Method	50.8	63.0	47.6	34.8	34.9	35.3	51.4

Source: National Family Health Survey, 1998-99.

Among Muslims; only 30.2 per cent of Muslim women were using any modern method, the prevalence rate for Hindus was 44.3 per cent and it was recorded as high as 63.9 per cent in case of women belonging to Buddhist religion. Again, condom and female sterilization rates were reported somewhat high as compared to other methods of contraception. However, female sterilization rate among Muslims has been reported just quite low i.e. 19.6 per cent as compared to female sterilization rate (36.2 per cent) among Hindu women. Unmet need for family planning among Muslim women has been found higher than the Hindu women. Moreover, 63.0 per cent Muslim women were reported not using any method. Thus, performance of family planning among Muslim has been observed lower than Hindu women.

Social Autonomy

The progress of a society largely depends upon the status of its women. Without studying the status of women, it is not possible to measure the advancement of a society. Again, the position of women differs from one society to another. Interestingly, the Muslim women are difficult to explain without making reference to the position given to them in the religious texts. The major sources in this regard are the *Quran*, the *Hadith* and *Shariat*. Importantly, status of Muslim women in a cross-cultural perspective varies from one Muslim country to another. It differs largely due to the difference in the type of political system and governance. Interestingly, in any society education is the most effective vehical for socialization, modernization and social change. However, the Muslims of India did not progress much in terms of modern education, attending schools outside their homes. Traditional outlook, poverty and backwardness are the primary reasons for educational backwardness among Muslim women in India. Moreover, the Muslim levels of autonomy among women have been reported to be quite low as compared to women belonging to other social groups (Table 4).

Importantly, the new religion Islam gave women many rights that were not available to women in other parts of the globe. The right to own property in their own name, to choose their marriage partners, to maintain their name after marriage, to inherit and bequeath property, and to manage their affairs independently etc., are such rights which were given to Muslim women. Moreover, Islam condemned the practice of female infanticide and

TABLE 4

Women's Autonomy Among Social Groups

	Hindu	*Muslim*	*Christian*	*Sikh*	*Jain*	*Buddhist*	*Other*
Percentage not involved in any decision-making.	9.6	10.7	5.8	2.4	9.8	4.6	4.9
Percentage involved in decision making							
(i) What to cook	85.2	82.8	88.0	93.6	84.3	89.7	89.1
(ii) Own health care	50.8	50.5	63.0	74.6	54.7	57.0	52.8
(iii) Purchasing of Jewellery etc.	52.4	48.1	65.6	72.5	55.9	58.7	61.7
(iv) Staying with her parents/ siblings	48.0	43.4	61.7	64.6	47.0	52.7	58.4
Percentage who do not need permission to							
(i) Go to the market	31.8	23.4	44.6	46.2	50.9	56.3	33.3
(ii) Visit friends/ relatives	24.6	19.0	35.6	25.6	39.8	38.7	31.0
Percentage with access to money	59.4	56.0	68.5	74.0	74.0	72.2	60.6

Source: National Family Health Survey, 1998-99.

urged Muslims to treat women with fairness and justice. Again, Holy *Quran* and the predictions of the Prophet places women to a dignified position in society having right to education, self expression and inheritance in the property of deceased father and husband. However, Islam does not accord a status of absolute equality to women keeping in view their physical infirmity, psychological make up leading to their unique situation. They should be respected as daughters, sisters, wives and mothers and be treated as a complementary part of their lives. Thus, Islam is basically a humanistic and egalitarian religion. However, the plight of Muslim women is not satisfactory in south Asian countries including India. Interestingly, the choice of Muslim women has been limited for getting male life partner due to the practice of the caste system, though there is no caste system in Islam but this is perhaps the impact of Hinduism. Dowry system also prevails among Muslims, which is responsible for the lower status of women. Moreover, many women remain unmarried throughout their life due to caste choice and poverty. Again, practices of divorce, polygamy, dower (mehr) etc. have placed women in a lower status (Seema Parveen, 2001).

Suggestions for Advancement

1. From the point of view of gender equality, there is an imperative need for direct involvement of women in the management of big enterprises. There is a need to introduce gender sensitivity at the project formulation stage as well as project implementation, both at the governmental and non-governmental levels.
2. It is the need of hour to design and implement programmes for women through community based organizations. Non-governmental organizations may be helpful in better targeting of the poor women by creating an environment in the community for sustainable development.
3. In the participatory development process supported by various voluntary organization, organizing as well as strengthening of women's groups may generate a new sense of dignity, confidence and economic independence to some extent.
4. A societal reorientation for gender just society would require a radical transformation through awareness on gender issues and sustained efforts of imparting training and education on various developmental activities. Women's own

perceptions about themselves also need to be changed; besides a positive role played by media and related organizations.

5. Developing first generation entrepreneurs, strengthening existing support system, and improving the performance of women entrepreneurs are some of the crucial points that should be focused. This can be successfully achieved through sustained support of various organizations for developing infrastructure and imparting training, skill and other EDPs. However, these programmes must focus on the following areas: (1) identifying and selecting the right type of entrepreneurs; (2)developing entreprenial behaviour/qualities to ensure better management of the unit; (3)linking viable projects with timely supply of production/raw materials and marketing channel and the area in which the project is to be set up; (4) preparation of project plans best suited to theentreprenial concern and the area in which the project is to be setup; (5)equipping the woman entrepreneurs with managerial competence to ensure effective management of the units; (6) to organize finance, infrastructure and implementation support to ensure successful running of business; (7) post-supervision to projects established to ensure proper understanding of problems being faced and their appropriate solution(Sengupta and Singh, 2001).

6. The contribution of women to many subsistence, home based, off farm or non-traditional activities should be upgraded through programme inputs, like training, credit, marketing etc. there is a

dire need of appreciating and understanding the links between the different roles of women and hence for a conscious articulation and policy to promote employment of women as well as the links between technology and women work opportunities.

7. Though the policy document (women policy) has detailed out women's rights to productive resources, their access to land, credit, finance, insurance etc., all these remain severely constrained. Moreover state women policy should be drafted and implemented in each state ensuring a higher allocation on the women development programmes. Importantly, women belonging to Muslims community should be focused for empowerment.
8. Participation of women in planning and decision-making still remains an area of neglect. The formal institution such as political parties, legislators, trade unions, cooperative, techno-bureaucracy, industry, trade and commerce reflect a very low level of participation of women particularly at more responsible positions. To resolve this problem and to initiate necessary policy initiatives, a comprehensive policy statement should be brought out both by the government and corporate sectors. This policy should focus on the reservation, entitlements and gender just equatous society.
9. An effective support mechanism is needed at the grass root level to ensure that policies of rights, entitlements and ownership of land are made sustainable.

REFERENCES

Bhatty, Z. (1976), "Status of Muslims women and social change," in BR Nanda (Ed) *Indian Women from Purdah to Modernity,* New Delhi, National Publishing House.

Encloe, C.H. (1973), *Ethnic Conflict and Political Development,* Boston, Little Brown & Co.

Gupta, O.P. (1983), Equality of Educational Opportunity and Muslims, *Muslim India,* November.

IIPS (1992-1993), National Family Health Survey, Bombay. International Institute of Population Sciences.

IIPS (1998-1999), National Family Health Survey, Bombay. International Institute of Population Sciences.

Imam (Ed.) (1975), *Muslim in India,* New Delhi, Orient Longman.

Latif, S. (1983), Report on the status of women in minority community: the case of Muslims in India, Delhi, and Govt. of India.

NCAER, (1999), *India Human Development Report,* Delhi, OUP.

Parkin, F., (1971), *Class Inequality and Political Order,* London, Macqubbon and Kee.

Parveen, S. (2001), *Muslims Women in Changing Context,* Lucknow, Ph.D. Thesis, Lucknow University.

Sengupta, A.K. and Singh, A.K. (2001), "Women empowerment: some issues and suggestions" in Surendra Singh and S.P. Srivastava (Ed), *Gender Equality Through Women's Empowerment: Strategies and Approaches,* Lucknow, Bharat Book Center.

13

INDIAN MUSLIM WOMEN AND PURDAH (VEILING)

—Abhilasha Srivastava

The most important factor limiting the role and status of Muslim women is purdah i.e. the physical screening of women by the wearing outer garment, which covers her from head to toe. It is claimed somewhat dubiously that the purdah is sanctioned by the *Koran*. The purdah is one of the significant customs in the Islamic culture. It has become an indispensable part of the Muslim social structure because a high status was attributed to such families in which women observed purdah. Prophet ordered the women of his family and tribe to use chadder while making public appearance in order to distinguish them from those of other families. Purdah conveys a variety of meanings: purdah of eyes refer to the lowering of eye lids, or looking with down cast eyes for women, and Muslim women in this particular context are not expected to look straight into the eyes of 'other' specially members of opposite sex. Similarly there is a purdah of 'voice' for women are not expected to talk in 'raised' voices, the softer spoken a woman is the more feminine she is supposed to be. The purdah between the zenana, the female quarters, and the mardana, male quarters segregates Muslim women as a category from men.

As the time passed this practice of elite family was taken up by other Muslim families too. Thus using chaddar becomes a status symbol and did not exclusively remain as a means of segregation of females, from males. There are several instances throughout the history in which we find that the females of Muslim elite class have been using purdah to maintain their identity and distinguish themselves from the other non-elite Muslim women.

Of those who observed purdah, most did not so constantly but a great many observe purdah when visiting relative or family despite the fact that purdah is a sign of upward mobility because only the rich upper class could afford to keep their in purdah. It also became a sign of class differentiation and was used by upward mobile groups. In India after independence these features were adopted by general masses, including the converted Muslims, who where aspiring for a high status. Thus the Indian Muslim women started using purdah in the form of burqa as their status symbol than a part of Islamic tradition.

On the other hand burqa has come to perform in recent years tell a reveling tale of socio-economic conditions of Muslims in walled city of Delhi. The burqa often reveals the affluence of the wearer when it is made of expensive imported cloth stitched by a tailor who is a burqa specialist. It equally lays bare the poverty of the wearer: a torn burqa stitched and re-stitched, often with patches here and there, reveals a lot. But it often helps to hide poverty of the wearer since it covers the torn and dirty clothes underneath. Similarly burqa is used to hide affluence when women, who normally do no wear burqa, wear it when they are dressed for a wedding and adorned with ornaments. Burqa is used as an instrument to hide and reveal property and affluence; itself as shown above is a symbol of socio-economic status of the wearer.

Apart from traditional roles the burqa performs, the present study revealed a new set of roles that it has acquired with the changing conditions, and exposure to certain modern trends, and certain new constraints.

The practice of seclusion of purdah has restricted movement of women. It has forced those Muslim women into a limited circular of interaction and has denied them opportunity to lean and function as mature and confident individual who are aware of there rights and privileges and can struggle to prevent their violation. The reasons for using burqa are related to their family tradition. Majority of women younger in age observe purdah not out of their own wish but due to their social surroundings and compulsion from parents. It is also true that parents are pressurized by family members, relatives and neighbors to put their daughters and females in purdah. Family tradition and few women by religious binding govern older women. A majority of those who do not observe purdah belong to nuclear family and are new settler in town. Yet such women support the practice of observing purdah by Muslim women and say that burqa is not truly in accordance with the Islamic sanction and therefore is an obstacle in the progress.

Sometimes the distinctions of purdah have an intriguing quality of interest. At the public meeting of the all Asian women's conference in Lahore held in university convocation hall the address of welcome was delivered from behind the screen by a distinguished women at the time still in purdah. The voice was amplified by the loud speakers, which gave any thing but the impression of purdah. This fact had special significance since in India strict purdah has required that a woman's voice should not be heard out of the harem.

Some of these illustrations may seem to be entirely illogical, distinctions without a difference but at least some are based on the rather fine distinction drawn between unveiling for business or impersonal reasons and unveiling as purely social matter. In the first case, lifting the veil for official context seems logical because based on necessity. The present period in some country is one of gradual evaluation between the so-called necessary unveiling and unveiling for merely personal reasons. But these various fine distinctions become more and more artificial and are at last ignored. Because of the many interesting exceptions to the uniform observance of the veil, it seems fair to conclude that after all, the restraint of the veil for the great majority is not a matter of religion but of custom. If it were matter of religion, it would make no difference whether the Lucknow begum were in Lucknow or Kashmir; or whether the Egyptian school principal were having a business conversation or a purely social visit. The veil would be retain in either case, regardless of place or extenuating circumstances, as religion has a certain permanent quality. Evidently, it is not religion, but the fear of public opinion, which prevents the lifting of the veil. The idea that "it just isn't done" seems to be the main deterrent.

As long as veiling is the conventional thing, unveiling will probably be regarded as not quite respectable and perhaps even actually immoral, since the conventional always bears the seal of being respectable and moral, whereas the strange and unconventional act is regarded with suspicion. As yet the veil bears the badge of respectability quite generally in the Muslim world. This may explain, at least partially while a lower class in each country is slower to change than the upper class, since the former always aspires to raising its social position, while the later can always afford to take the social risk. Here (in India) for example, having one's wife in purdah is regarded as a certain social distinction. The Indian cook aspires to the same degree of purdah for his wife as the butler can afford. Hence as soon as the cook gets raise in wages for a little bit, he promptly puts his wife in purdah and feels that he has climbed up on rung on the social ladder. This idea that the purdah is the mark of social distinction reaches far down in the social scale, and only stops at the lowest economic levels were it becomes impossible. Coming out of purdah, naturally and very fortunately has begun in the upper class in each country and by the law of imitation is working down. Unveiling of all classes comes mere easily if the life styles have been set up at the top. Since this case, the importance in each country of unveiled leaders such as Madame Sharawi pasha in Cairo, Begum Hamid Ali in Baroda, Mrs. Tyabji in Bombay and Lady Shafi and lady Abdul Kadir in Lahore, is very great, since they represent wealth and social prestige, and hence, invite imitation. It is also observed that there is a world of difference between the mask-like, shapeless Indian burqa and the chic modernized Charshaf and veil in Syria, or the alluring white chiffon veil in Egypt, which leaves the eyes, entirely free. There is corresponding difference in the freedom of personality, which these different types of veiling permit. In all Muslim countries except India the veil has passed through various stages, which represent a gradual departure from the spirit as well as the letter of religious tradition and indicate a growing style consciousness or urge to display some feminine charm. The Indian burqa has offered no such satisfying possibilities as the modish pelerine, or filmy veil and draped toque. But even though these various forms of the veil differ widely in their degree of concealment, they all alike constitute a certain barrier between the women and outside the world. Even though the pecheh in Iran has ceased entirely to cover the face and the Cairo chiffon could not be more revealing, the subtle nuance of separation remains.

A veil however high or low, thick or thin remains the veil, with its full meaning until it disappears. It is never just a piece of black or white chiffon, or merely a special type of garment. It is never causally assumed or laid aside without reflection. It presents strange paradoxes. It is restrictive emphasis on sex relationship and also on moral protection; a sign of utter dependence and also of freedom from responsibility; a handicap to real progress and a symbol of special privilege. In a word the veil represents an entirely different social system. Discarding it therefore involves a whole change of psychology. As long as any vestige of the veil remain, system has not more changed.

One might perhaps imagine that all Muslim women are eager to lift the veil. But such is by no means the case with many Muslims specially those of the older generation. Unveiling for them was feared as a real calamity, their life and thought is centered in the purdah. They regard the veil as a part of their religion. The religious element seems less vital elsewhere, but all through the Muslim east religion has colored the thinking the older generation. An even stronger reason for these aversion to unveiling is the sense of unfamiliarity which even the thought of unveiling gives them they are entirely at home with the veil and mistress of situation. Furthermore unveiling seems to them full of moral dangers, as their life has been centered on a morality based entirely on the protection of the barriers. These older women represent a stronger conservative opposition in each country against lifting the veil.

Some Muslim women, also of the older group, would hesitate to give up the veil or charshaf not merely because of the moral protection, the need for which is very much emphasized but also because of freedom from responsibility afforded by the veil. Such freedom may seem paradoxical but it is true that, that a veiled woman is not a personality to be criticized for individual action, she is merely a massed figure whom no one recognizes.

An unusual role of burqa is to hide the identity of prostitutes, both Muslim and non-Muslim. But the strong perfume they use helps the customer to identify them. For most people however they would appear to be ordinary burqa clad women. Another interesting use of burqa: that girls for cheating in examination hall, copying can be possible under the cover of their burqa.

Aside from the older group who cling to the veil there is in every country a large number of women of upper class who are more or less satisfied with the comfortable protected life of seclusion, free from responsibility, enjoying complete liberty in their own limited sphere, and a certain amount of prestige. Unveiling world involve a good deal of readjustment, a new technique of living. They prefer the familiar world to which they are accustomed. They already adopted European clothes, have bobbed hair perhaps and even a mercel wave and are satisfied with these measures of modernity, they may be intellectually prepared to unveil, but the veil does not seem a vital matter. There is no keen sense of what they have lacked and hence, no urge or change. They regard unveiling as a possibility but on the whole are indifferent to change. A fairly large number of women, however recognize a fundamental handicap in connection to veil. Individually they would not decide to lift the veil and thus incur family opposition or public criticism, but they would become a general change.

A good many Iranian women had hoped for an order

from the Shah. In Iraq one heard frequently the wish of Kamal Ataturk to end the system of the veil, before the rapid changes of the past winter.

Although the great majority of women are passive in their attitude concerning the veil, but willing to change eventually, there is an active minority of women who have unveiled and are working steadily against the veil. These regard it as a root evil, as a Muslim woman in Calcutta diagnosed it "carbonmonooxide which causes slow death". An Iranian woman expressed the handicap of the veil as keeping women always "prisoners to sex". The younger generation, always without exception, belong with this group. Perhaps many of the graduates of the school and colleges returning to their conservative homes may accept the veil without open revolt, because of the differential attitude of young for age in the east, but there is a deep sense of dissatisfaction. As a young school in Tripoli said "our mothers and grandmothers are happy with the veil and harem, but with us it is different. We know that there is a different kind of life and will not be satisfied until we have it". Another young Muslim girl eager for freedom but living in the conservative atmosphere said, " every time we hear of the death of an old person, we praise god that there is no less conservative. Al-Hamdullah".

As to the attitude of man towards discarding the veil, the great majority is not committed to the idea. Education for girls has been expected as necessary, but not unveiling. The masculine reaction to lifting the veil ranges from active opposition to on difference. The ultra-conservative, specially religious leaders, base there opposition on religious principle but one often has the feeling that few are really impelled by religion to oppose the veil. By far the greater is actuated by a feeling protective possession of the women in their families and satisfaction with the status quo, which ensures their authority. Often the highly protected attitude is explained on the bases of the moral insecurity of the invalid Muslim women. "The times are yet not ripe; men's moral are too low"; " the general public is not yet prepared for women's freedom are the oft-repeated refrain. Doubtless there is much truth but also a good deal of alibi in these reasons given against unveiling. This idea of the need for protection in the view of brothers expressed as: "I cannot allow my beautiful sister to be exposed to the gaze of common people."

Burqa has undergone drastic changes in different countries in different centuries. It will not be possible to elaborate the history of burqa in this brief paper. I will rather concentrate on some of the changes that I have observed in the city of Lucknow in recent years. A number of factors can be attributed to these changes. Firstly, interaction with the neighboring countries has not only changed the texture and design of the burqa, but changes are also visible in the colors and prints coming into vogue in recent years. Some studies have been intended that the burqa is the symbol of low socio-economic status and backwardness of Muslims in general. However, the study reveals that although the above observations may be true to a large extent, yet the number and variety of burqas one possesses may also be an indication of one's economic status. The burqa, which till a couple of years ago, generally confined of 2 colors, black and white and was generally of cotton cloth, was informally designed; the white burqa was stitched in the shuttle-cock design whereas the black was in 2 parts, the cloak and the veil, which could either be made out of cotton cloth or satin. Women themselves stitched these two types of burqa. But these types have gradually gone out of vogue. Burqa-stitching is gradually becoming specialization. And one can witness a large number of shops, which sells material for burqa.

Another visible change is the introduction of the chadder, a wrap around, like a shawl, which is often beautifully embroidered or is a longish piece of printed cloth (synthetic) very popular in Pakistan and most often imported from this neighboring country. Within these trends there are a number of variations. Often the burqa covers the body as well as the face.

Sometimes it covers the body and not the face and most interesting of all the varieties was the burqa which neither covers the body nor the face. And finally the burqa, which revealed or rather accentuated the profile of the wearer rather than concealing it. This reveals how the burqa has come to acquire new functions, which contradict the very spirit with which it was first introduced.

Commensurate with the rapid changes taking place in society burqa has come to play various new functions. As mentioned above often the burqa is made of cloth that clings to the body of wearer; it is stitched in such a manner that it accentuates the beauty of wearer. The veil is made of very fine material behind which the immaculately painted face of the wearer becomes even more attractive.

The use of burqa is however related to education and age of persons than to their family structure and duration of stay in a particular urban locale. It has become more a status symbol in Muslim families of certain social and economic standings and is not a part of the Islamic culture. It has been seen that in present days educated women are not using it in compared to any uneducated women. Non-observance of parda in form of burqa or chadder has helped the women to take advantages of certain crashing conditions and enjoy freedom seems to be correct even in the urban locale. It has been observed that such respondents who do not use burqa are more liberal in their outlook as well as they have more representation in employment. Even a majority of those who observed it do not put it on when they go out of their home.

The sanction of purdah seems rooted in religion and family practice. Not surprisingly, the prevalence of purda is highest in traditionally Muslim-dominated states like U.P., Andhra Pradesh (Hyderabad), Kashmir, West Bengal and Delhi. These areas are also traditionally conservative with regard to women, irrespective of community. Some women who discard felt this was out of question from a personal point of view others felt that the husband would constitute a barrier. This seems to imply a closer and more understanding relationship between husband and wife. It also indicates the recognition by the husband that the need for seclusion of women is not as great as it is used to be.

Of those who observed for religious reasons, the majority would not allow their daughters to discard it; but others said that they would have no objection. While purda has been a major factor in the subjugation of women, economic pressure have made it necessary for Muslim girls, particularly in urban areas to be educated; the observance of purda as a result have been more flexible (the purdah is often discarded outside the limits of area in which they live and donned again on the way home). Thus it can be said that the Muslim family is changing under the present economic and social situation, from its traditional joint structure, autocratic nature and with women's ascribed role to nuclear family structure. The women's ascribed role in it is also replaced by their achieved role. The education and age of the women are responsible to modify their role patterns in the families. Though most of the Muslim families continue even today to be patriarchal women enjoy better position in the family of which they were deprived a generation ago. Education gives them opportunity to think rationally on the different aspects of equality in present time. The younger generation is more aware of sharing the family responsibility. In other words the Muslim women are now able to understand the present socio-economic situation and they try to play an important family responsibility by joining hands with the male members in the family. In most of the families women observe purdah but there are some very old Muslim women who are coming forward and fighting for the cause of taking higher education and are very progressive in behaviour. Still they are afraid of the community leaders regarding observance of purdah.

It presents few spectacular evidences of advance but rather a general outward movement from the home towards some measure of participation in business and personal life. In some places and along certain lines the signs of change are quit definite; in others securely perceptible, merely like straws that show which way the wind blows. This movement toward economic independence has affected principally the educated upper middle classes, and is slowly producing a type similar to a business and professional women in the west. But as yet there are practically no changes among the less well-educated classes of the girls, whom one would except to find in many types of employment, which constitute in the western world the great majority of employed women and girls. In all of these fields of women's work Muslim women are conspicuous for their absence, such as shops, all kinds of offices, beautiful parlors, telegraph and telephone offices, restaurants and theaters—in fact the hundred and one of the ordinary type of women's work. From all these lines of employment the veil successfully debars Muslim women of the middle and lower class.

It is probably because education and social change are more retarded in these classes than in the upper class, that the economic status of these groups is also changing slowly. But the general spirits of conservatism in the east with regard to women in employment widens for the non-Muslim women is taking place within the limits of veil, but until the veil lifts, one can scarcely accept a full and natural measure of economic life. In the mean time just water dropping steadily on a stone gradually wears down the surface, each individual Muslim women entering a new profession slowly wears down in her community the traditional Muslim prejudice against economic independence for women.

REFERENCES

Asghar Ali Engineer, *Women in the Changing Islamic System*, New Delhi, India, 1987.

Brijbhusan, Jamila, *Muslim Women: In Purdah and out of it*, New Delhi, 1980.

Dube, Leela, *Matriliny and Islam: Religion and Society in The Laccadives*, 1969.

Hyder, Quratulain, "Muslim Women in India," in Devaki Jain (Ed.), *Indian Women*, New Delhi, 1975.

Maudoodi, A.A., *Purdah and Status of Women in Islam*, Lahore, 1972.

Mohini Anjum, *Behind Burqa*, New Delhi, India, 1992.

Mohini Anjum, *"Muslim Women in India"'* New Delhi, India (Edi.), 1992.

Talat Ara Ashrafi, *"Muslim Women in Changing Perspective,"* New Delhi, India, 1992.

Woodsmall, Ruth Frances, *Women in Changing Islamic System*, New Delhi, India, 1983.

14

POPULATION GROWTH AND FERTILITY OF MUSLIM COMMUNITY IN INDIA

—S.R. Rastogi

The study of population growth on the basis of religious composition would appear to be irrelevant to many in secular country like India but social scientists and demographers recognize the significance of religion and culture in influencing the demographic condition. The knowledge of the relationship between religious affiliation and fertility is considered to be important for the programme of population control and promotion of socio-economic welfare of the people belonging to different religious communities. Large family size and fastly growing population increase the incidence of poverty and aggravate problems of unemployment, poor health and educational backwardness in different social groups and communities. India is a multi-religious nation and in the total population of the country 82 per cent are Hindus, 12 per cent Muslims, 2 per cent Christians and the rest 4 per cent Sikhs, Buddhists and Jains. At present the country is passing through the second stage of demographic transition (low mortality and declining birth rates) and significant fertility differentials have emerged between various religious communities, particularly among Hindus and Muslims. The demographic surveys conducted in other countries have demonstrated that the level of fertility is higher in most Muslim populations mainly because the children are highly valued in Islamic culture and the use of contraceptives is deemed to be un-Islamic (Swee-Hock, 1989, Anwar M. and Shah Nasran M., 1986, Shah and Shah, 1984, Nagi and Stockwell, 1982).

Main objective of the present paper is to examine the trends in population growth of the Muslims, considered as the largest minority community in India and to compare such trends with the rates of population growth among Hindus of the country. It has also been tried to study the Hindu-Muslim differentials in the preferences for ideal number of children, levels of fertility and contraceptive acceptance. The analysis is based on the secondary data collected from the Census of India, National Family Health Surveys: 1992-93 and 1998-99 and some other important surveys conducted by different official agencies.

Population Growth

The proportions of the population of Hindus and Muslims in total population of the country during 1961 to 1991 are given in Table 1. The data for 2001 Census based on the religious groups are not yet available. The table shows that percentage of Muslims in total population of India increased from 10.7 per cent in 1961 to 12.1 per cent in 1991 while the proportion of Hindus has declined from 83.5 per cent to 82 per cent during the same period. It has further been noticed from the table that during the previous decades, the decennial rate of population growth has been significantly higher for the Muslims as compared to Hindu community. During 1981-91, the population of Muslims increased by 31 per cent as against 23 per cent of Hindu population. During this decade the total population of India increased by 23.9 percent. This indicates that the rate of population growth for Muslim community has been higher than the national increase while for Hindus it has been lower.

TABLE 1

Population Growth of Hindus and Muslims in India

Indicators	*Hindus*	*Muslims*
Percentage to total Population of India:		
1961	83.5	10.7
1971	82.7	11.2
1981*	82.6	11.4
1991**	82.0	12.1
Percentage decadal Growth rate:		
1961-71	23.7	30.9
1971-81*	24.1	30.7
1981-91**	23.0	31.4
Percentage decadal Growth rate for Population of India:		
1971-81	24.7	
1981-91	23.9	

* Excludes Assam

** Excludes Jammu and Kashmir.

Source: Registrar General, India, Census of India, 1981-91.

In Uttar Pradesh, the percentage of Muslim population to total population of the state is higher (15.9 per cent in 1981 and 17.3 per cent in 1991) as compared to percentage of the Muslims in total population of the country (11.4 per cent in 1981 and 12.1 per cent in 1991). The rate of population growth for Muslim community of the state has also been higher than Hindus during the previous decades (Table 2). During 1981-91 the decadal rate of population growth was 23.1 per cent for Hindus as against 36.5 per cent for Muslims in the state of Uttar- Pradesh. With a view to understand the major reasons for higher rate of population growth of a community, it is imperative to study the reproductive goals, fertility levels and the practice of family planning methods among the couples.

TABLE 2

Population Growth of Hindus and Muslims in Uttar Pradesh

Indicators	*Hindus*	*Muslims*
Population : 1981	92,365,968	17,657,735
1991	113,712,829	24,109,684
Percentage to total Population of the state:		
1981	83.3	15.9
1991	81.7	17.3
Percentage decadal Growth rate:		
1971-81	24.8	29.1
1981-91	23.1	36.5
Percentage decadal Growth rate for Population of state:		
1971-81	25.5	
1981-91	25.5	

Source: Directorate of Census Operations, Uttar Pradesh, Census of India, 1991.

Ideal Number of Children

The socio-economic groups to which couples belong generally shape their reproductive goals or attitudes towards ideal family size. Fertility preferences and perceptions relating to ideal number of children which are more or less governed by religious and cultural norms among the couples with traditional values, are significant determinants of their actual or achieved family size. The findings of the National Family Health Surveys conducted in India during 1992-93 and 1998-99 reveal that Muslim couples of the country consider larger number of children as ideal for a family than Hindu couples. In both of these surveys mean ideal number of children was noticed as more than three for Muslim couples and less than three for Hindus (Table 3).

TABLE 3

Reproductive Goals and Fertility Levels among Hindu and Muslim Couples in India

Indicators	*Hindus*		*Muslims*	
	1992-93	*1998-99*	*1992-93*	*1998-99*
Mean ideal number of Children:	2.8	2.6	3.3	3.1
Mean number of Children ever born (A):	4.8	4.3	5.8	5.7
Total Fertility Rate (B):	3.3	2.8	4.4	3.6

A— Mean number of children ever born to ever-married women age 40-49 years.

B— For women age 15-49.

Source: 1. National Family Health Survey (*India*): 1992-93.
2. National Family Health Survey (*India*): 1998-99.

A study conducted by the State Institute of Health and Family Welfare, Lucknow in the selected districts of Uttar Pradesh shows that Muslim couples living in the rural Muslim dominated areas opted for the highest number of children (4.3) as constituting an ideal family as compared to those living in rural Hindu dominated and urban areas

(Singh, Saxena and Gupta, 1996). Among Muslim couples, those who are educated and have modern way of living, largely prefer small family size (Sharma, 1994).

Child Bearing

A survey conducted by the office of the Registrar General, India covering rural and urban households of the country, demonstrates higher level of fertility among Muslims as compared to other religious groups (Registrar General, India, 1979). For rural areas of the country the birth rate was 35.2 and total fertility rate 5.1 for the Muslims as compared to 32.8 and 4.5 respectively for the Hindus.

The findings of the National Family Health Surveys as presented in Table: 3 reveal that Muslims have considerably higher fertility than the Hindus. During 1998-99 the total fertility rate was 3.6 for Muslim women as compared to 2.8 for Hindus. Mean number of children ever born to ever-married women aged 40-49 years was found as 5.7 for Muslims as against 4.3 for Hindus (1998-99). The level of fertility is higher among Muslims largely due to religious orthodoxy which prevails among poor, less educated and socially backward (Sharma- 1994). However, the researchers suggest that Islam has a non-supportive attitude towards fertility control (Rob, 1992).

Practice of Family Planning Methods

During 1980 the Operations Research Group, Baroda conducted All India Family Planning Survey which shows that the disapproval of family planning was highest among Muslims. The proportion of couples who disapproved family planning was 33 per cent among Muslims as against 16 per cent among Hindus (Operations Research Group, 1980). The practice of family planning methods was also lower among Muslims (23 per cent as current users) than

Hindus (36 per cent as current users).

TABLE 4

Percentage of Women* Currently Using any Family Planning Method among Hindus and Muslims in India

Indicators	*Hindus*		*Muslims*	
	1992-93	*1998-99*	*1992-93*	*1998-99*
Currently using any method of family planning:	41.6	49.2	27.7	37.0
Currently using any modern method of family planning:	37.7	44.3	22.0	30.2
Not using any method:	58.4	50.8	72.3	63.0

* Currently married women.

Source: As in Table 3.

The data collected in the National Family Health Surveys reveal that in India during 1998-99 the proportion of current users of any method of family planning was 49 per cent among Hindus as against 37 per cent among Muslims. The percentage of those who were currently using any modern method of planning was also lower among Muslims than Hindus during 1992-93 as well as 1998-99 were not using any contraceptive method (Table 4).

A survey conducted during 1994 in the selected villages of Lucknow district shows that religious faith is one of the major barriers to the adoption of family planning methods among Muslim women. In the villages covered under the study, none of the interviewed women among Hindus avoided the use of birth control devices due to religious faith while among Muslims 34 per cent did not use methods due to their belief that family planning contradicts with their religion (Rastogi, 1996). In the context of family planning and Islam it has been pointed out (Khan, 1978,

Bhatia, 1990) that "Islam forbids abortion and all permanent family planning methods. However, several Ulemas permitted it on grounds of health". Many Muslims feel that "a sterilized man cannot perform *namaz* (prayer) and he is not allowed to go for *Haj* (pilgrimage to Mecca and Madina)" (Sharma, 1994). Such perceptions lead to anti-family planning attitudes which raise the level of fertility. These attitudes against family planning continue to be cause of concern and are to be changed through effective counseling techniques.

Conclusion

The preceding analysis reveals that during the previous decades the population of the Muslim community has been growing at the faster rate than that of the Hindus. Muslim couples have higher level of fertility and the practice of family planning methods has been much lower among them than Hindus. Majority of the Muslim couples (63 percent) in the country are not using any family planning method. The analysis suggests that effective strategy should be developed to reduce fertility among the Muslims through their community leaders who should be properly convinced and educated about the significance of the small family norm and advantages of the family planning methods. The health and family welfare workers should be properly trained in effective counseling techniques to remove misconceptions and anti-family planning attitudes in the Muslim community. At the same time intensive efforts are needed to raise socio-economic and educational status of the Muslim people so that they would develop rational attitudes towards child bearing and contraception.

REFERENCES

Anwar M. and Shah Nasra M, *Basic Needs, Women and Development: A Survey of Squatters in Lahore, Pakistan,* East-West Center, Honolulu and International Development Research Center, Ottawa, 1986.

Bhatia, P.S., "Population Growth of Various Communities in India: Myth and Reality" *Demography India,* Vol. 19, No. 1, Jan.-June 1990.

Khan, M.E. "Is Islam against family planning?" in *Birth Control Among Muslims in India,* Manmohan Publications, 1978.

Nagi, M.H. and E.G., Stockwell, "Muslim Fertility: Current trends and Future outlook" *Journal of South Asian and Middle East Studies,* Vol. 6, No. 48, 1982.

Operations Research Group, Baroda, *Family Planning Practice in India,* Second All India Survey, 1980.

Rastogi, S.R., *Operations Research on Spacing Methods (A Diagnostic Study Conducted in Lucknow District),* Series: B, Survey Report No. 49, Population Research Centre, University of Lucknow, 1996.

Registrar General India, Ministry of Home Affairs, Government of India, *Survey on Infant and Child Mortality* (A preliminary report), New Delhi, 1979.

Rob, A.K., Ubaidur "Socio-economic Determinants of Fertility: What do we Know", *Demography India,* Vol. 21, No. 1, Jan.-June 1992.

Shah Nasra M and Shah Makhdoom A., " From Non-use to use: Prospects of Contraceptive adoption", in Alam I. And Dinesen B. (Edi.) *Fertility in Pakistan: A Review of Findings from the Pakistan Fertility Survey,* Voorburg, Netherlands: International Statistical Institute, 1984.

Sharma, A.K., "Muslim Fertility in Urban U.P.: A qualitative study," *Demography India,* Vol. 23, No. 1 & 2, Jan.-December 1994.

Singh R.P., A.K. Saxena and R.B. Gupta, "Muslim Fertility: Influence of Community Dominance", *The Journal of Family Welfare,* Vol. 42, No. 4, December 1996.

Swee-Hock Saw, "Muslim Fertility Transition: The case of the Singapore, Malays" *Asia-Pacific Population Journal,* Vol. 4, No. 3, September 1989.

15

EDUCATIONAL DEVELOPMENT AMONG MUSLIM WOMEN: EMERGING PERSPECTIVE AND TRENDS

—Seema Parveen

Education at various levels, primary, secondary and higher, and in various forms: formal and non-formal, general and professional is a major tool for economic changes that would lead to raising a person achieving the education above the poverty level and thereby reducing the high poverty percentage of the country. It does this mainly by making men and women, boys and girls employable through equipping them with various skills. There are, however, other counterparts essential for the successful employment of the tools of economic change provided by education, such as increasing investment in agriculture and industry particularly small industry, updating techniques and technologies there is ensuring that there are increasing employment intensive occupation and continuous appraising, highlighting and countering of the inequalities of the society, only if these pre-conditions are met. Education will be an effecting tool for economic change for the individual family and society.

Education at the primary and elementary level is the

most effective tool for bringing about macro and micro-economic changes in any society. It is a major tool for alleviation of poverty. Moreover, higher and professional education is the most direct contributor to the economic betterment. The relationship between education, productivity and income has been established much earlier. Interestingly, literature learning is also producing social changes in making the women conscious of their rights, enabling them to organize to fight various socials evils like the sale of arrack, dowry demands and the violence against women.

In India, education is also a very important part of social and cultural life. Women education has always been a priority area and the entire education system to work for women's education and empowerment. At the time of independence, India's education system was not only small but also characterized by intra and inter-religion, as well as structural imbalances. As education is linked with the totality of the development process, several articles in the Constitutions emphasized certain key principles, which would underline the educational system in the country.

Since Independence provision of educational opportunities for women has been an important component of the national endeavours. Though these endeavours did yield significant results, gender disparities persist with a compromising tenacity, more so in rural areas among disadvantaged communities. The National Policy on Education (NPE) 1986 updated in 1992 is a landmark in Indian Education. It perceived education as an agent that could bring about basic change in the status of women. To quote, in order to neutralize the accumulated distortions of the part, there will be a well-conceived edge in favour of women. The National education system will play a positive interventionist role in the employment of women, the removal of women's illiteracy and obstacles inhibiting their access to retention in, elementary education will receive over-riding priority through provision of special support services, setting of time targets and effective monitoring.

Today, participation of girls is considerably lower than that of boys and drop-out rates are in variously higher. Gender sensitivity should be the concern in designing and implementing basic education programs to become more meaningful available to girls and women. Despite government efforts at universalization of elementary education half the Indian adult population continues to be illiterate and two-thirds of women are illiterate. Table 1 shows the illiteracy rate of Uttar Pradesh during 1951 to 2001. It is a startling fact that female's literacy is significantly lower than men.

TABLE 1

Literacy Rate: 1951-2001, Uttar Pradesh

Year	*Persons*	*Male*	*Females*
1951	12.02	19.17	4.07
1961	20.87	32.08	8.36
1971	23.99	35.01	11.23
1981	32.65	46.65	16.74
1991	40.71	54.82	24.37
2001	57.36	70.23	42.98
India			
2001	65.38	75.85	54.16

Source: Census 2001.

Education among Muslim Women

Education is the key instrument for women's development. The basic quality of women's education should be intellectual dynamic, which finally results in national dynamism. Islam attaches great values to education and enjoins upon every woman as well as to acquire knowledge fundamentally Islam has always considered learning at least a useful accessory to begin a good Muslim, and as necessary condition which helps to develop their faculties. The four things, which the prophet commands his followers to do for their children are: to circumcise them, to inform them of the principles of their religion; to educate them properly; and to marry them off when they reach the proper age. Traditional education pattern in Muslim society is largely religious in orientation and includes reading of the Quran and learning of Urdu secular education may be imparted either at home or at school.

National Policy of Education-1986 states the following regarding education of minorities in its document: some minority groups are educationally deprived or backward. Greater attention will be paid to the education of these groups in the interest of equality and social justice. This will naturally include the constitutional guaranties given to them to establish and administer their own educational institutions and protection to their languages and Culture.

The scenario of education among Indian Muslims is depressing and disheartening. The causes are not far to seek globally; the last centuries have witnessed the phenomenon of Muslim, withdrawal and stagnation. Moreover, the standard of teaching in Muslim schools and colleges, with some exception is indifferent. Their results are often poor and sometimes it is the non-Muslim students enrolled who prevent the average from going down further. Again, Muslim parents by and large, adopt an attitude of non-challenge towards their children's education. Those parents who are educated but their number is not large, have little time or inclination for helping out their children with the homework. Those who are uneducated or illiterate have of course an excuse. This results in Muslim students being deprived of the environment and guidance so necessary in their early stages of education.

Among Muslims in urban areas artisan and petty traders predominate. They tend to make their children supplement their income at a very early age by working in the family profession, depend them in the process of the benefits of education. Moreover, for various reasons the share that Muslims have in employment both in public and private sectors is ridiculously low. This has served as a great disincentive to education for their children [Hamid 1986].

There is no controversy about the fact that Muslims of India are a backward community whatever criteria one may employ to identify the overall backwardness of the community. There is, however, a controversy regarding the reasons of this backwardness; the blame is attributed to Muslim's mentality of defeatism and motivational deficit [Hasan 2000].

Gopal Krishan had conducted a study of Muslim's attitude and there place in Indian society during 1973-74. As the study was sponsored by the ministry of Home Affairs, its findings are not available but Saxena [1983] revealed that Gopal Krishan found that educational level of Muslims is lower and dropout rate is higher in all parts of India and in every economic category. This state of backwardness of Muslims has been found to prevail even in Muslim managed schools and colleges where there is no possibility of discrimination against them. A survey of Muslim managed schools and colleges shows that there was dropout from 83.8 per cent enrolment percentage at school level to 40.4 per cent at the college level. As many as 14 reasons of this state of affair are listed by Shah [1984] who conducted the study.

Although, religion and caste have an impact on many types of social behaviour in India, such as opting for a secular education normally imparted by public institutions. STs and SCs recorded a literacy rate of about 40 per cent in comparison have the highest level of literacy of about 81 per cent. Muslims on the contrary have literacy level of about 50 per cent. While female literacy is significantly low for all social groups. (Table 2)

TABLE 2

Literacy Rates (Percentage) and Gender Disparity by Social Groups

Social Groups	*Person*	*Male*	*Female*	*F/M*
STs	39.3	51.4	26.0	0.51
SCs	41.5	53.4	28.2	0.53
Hindus	53.3	65.9	39.2	0.60
Muslims	49.4	59.5	38.0	0.64
Christians	80.8	85.0	76.5	0.90
Other Minorities	53.8	62.9	43.8	0.70

Note: Literacy Rates (aged 7 & above)

Source: Indian Human Development Report, 1999.

Table 3 also shows that high literacy rate have been found more pronouncing among Christians and Hindus while Muslims are lagging behind in terms of achieving educational level of matriculation and above. National Family Health Survey, 1998-99 also reveals that 60.5 per cent Muslim women are illiterate and hardly 9 per cent women are above high school. This is also to be noted that educational levels among Muslim women are lower than educational levels among other social groups.

TABLE 3

Proportion of Population Completing Middle and Matriculation level Education by Social Groups

Social Groups	*Middle level (aged 15 & above)*				*Matric level (aged 17 & above)*			
	Persons	*Male*	*Female*	*F/M*	*Persons*	*Male*	*Female*	*F/M*
STs	9.2	12.7	5.4	0.43	4.9	7.3	2.3	0.31
SCs	10.1	14.6	5.1	0.35	4.9	7.3	2.3	0.31
Hindus	13.0	16.9	8.6	0.51	8.5	12.0	4.7	0.39
Muslims	12.0	15.8	7.6	0.48	5.9	8.3	3.2	0.38
Christians	21.2	22.5	19.9	0.88	18.7	19.0	18.4	0.97
Other Minorities	12.3	15.7	8.6	0.55	11.5	15.3	7.3	0.48

Source: India Human Development Report, 1999.

This part of the paper is based on primary data collected through field survey in Lucknow district during 1997-98, covering a sample of 364 household.

TABLE 4

Age-wise Educational Status of Respondents

Age Group	*Illite-rate*	*Lite-rate*	*Prim-ary*	*J.H. School*	*High School*	*Inter*	*Grad-*	*P.G. & Above*	*Total*
Upto 25	4 (4.55)	—	4 (4.55)	6 (6.82)	14 (15.91)	12 (13.63)	40 (45.45)	8 (9.09)	88 (100.00)
26-35	8 (5.97)	14 (10.45)	4 (2.98)	10 (7.46)	28 (20.90)	10 (7.46)	44 (32.84)	16 (11.94)	134 (100.00)
36-45	12 (14.63)	14 (29.27)	4 (4.88)	8 (9.76)	6 (7.32)	10 (12.19)	12 (14.63)	6 (7.32)	82 (100.00)
46-55	—	14 (36.84)	2 (5.26)	2 (5.26)	8 (21.06)	2 (5.26)	—	10 (26.32)	38 (100.00)
55 -above	2 (9.09)	12 (54.55)	—	2 (9.09)	—	—	—	6 (27.27)	22 (100.00)
Total	26 (7.14)	64 (17.85)	14 (3.85)	28 (7.69)	56 (15.39)	34 (9.34)	96 (26.37)	46 (12.64)	364 (100.00)

Age-wise Educational Status of Respondents (Table 4) that more than one-fourth were found graduates while 18 per cent females were illiterate. Again, 15.39 per cent women were educated up to high school and 12.64 per cent respondents were educated up to post graduation level. In the age group of below 25 years, a large proportion of respondents were reported to be graduates while 16 per cent females were educated up to high school and about 14 per cent respondents were also reported to be educated up to inter level. Against this, in the age group of 36-45 years a high proportion of respondents was reported to be illiterate while about 15 per cent respondents were found graduates. In the age group of 46-55 years a majority of females were belonging to literate category while 26.32 per cent of interviewed women were found post-graduate. Again, more than half respondents in the age group of above 55 years was found literate while 27.27 per cent respondents were post-graduates. Thus, the overall picture emerges that in the low age group women were more educated and especially in higher education as compared to middle and upper age groups of respondents.

It is interesting to know that educational achievement of the respondent and the changed attitude towards necessity of women education, objective of their education etc., is very much affected by the education and occupation of respondents father and socio-economic status of the family and the structure of their family.

Again, Table 5 shows that percentage of children in higher education was reported higher in case of highly educated respondents. It is clear that highly educated women are more conscious regarding enrolment of their children in higher education.

TABLE 5

Education-wise Educational Level of Children of Respondents

Educational Level	*Male*	*Female*	*Total*	*Govt. School*	*Private*	*Nursery*	*Primary*	*J.H. School*	*High School*	*Inter*	*Graduate*	*P.G.*
Illiterate	26 (56.52)	20 (43.48)	46 (100.00)	24 (52.17)	22 (47.83)	4 (8.70)	14 (30.43)	14 (30.43)	4 (8.70)	6 (13.4)	4 (8.70)	—
Literate	66 (52.38)	60 (47.62)	126 (100.00)	84 (66.67)	42 (33.33)	6 (4.76)	38 (30.16)	20 (15.87)	22 (17.46)	14 (11.11)	22 (17.46)	4 (3.18)
Primary	14 (70.00)	6 (30.00)	20 (100.00)	14 (70.00)	6 (30.00)	4 (20.00)	6 (30.00)	4 (20.00)	2 (10.00)	210	2 (10.00)	—
J.H. School	30 (46.87)	34 (53.13)	64 (100.00)	36 (56.25)	28 (43.75)	10 (15.63)	16 (25.00)	10 (15.63)	8 (12.50)	6 (9.37)	14 (21.87)	—
High School	36 (35.29)	66 (64.71)	102 (100.00)	38 (37.25)	64 (62.75)	20 (19.61)	32 (31.37)	18 (17.65)	12 (11.76)	14 (13.73)	4 (3.92)	2 (1.96)
Inter	44 (56.41)	34 (43.59)	78 (100.00)	26 (33.33)	52 (66.67)	6 (7.69)	18 (23.08)	8 (10.26)	18 (23.08)	8 (10.26)	16 (20.51)	4 (5.12)
Graduate	48 (51.06)	46 (48.94)	94 (100.00)	24 (25.53)	70 (74.47)	18 (19.15)	22 (23.40)	10 (10.64)	26 (27.66)	6 (6.38)	10 (10.64)	2 (2.13)
P.G.	36 (55.88)	30 (44.12)	68 (100.00)	18 (26.47)	50 (73.53)	10 (14.71)	6 (8.82)	16 (23.53)	6 (8.82)	6 (8.82)	18 (26.48)	6 (8.8)
Total	302 (50.50)	296 (49.50)	598 (100.00)	264 (44.15)	334 (55.85)	78 (13.04)	152 (25.42)	100 (16.72)	98 (16.39)	62 (10.37)	90 (15.05)	18 (13.01)

TABLE 6

Vocational Training of Respondents

Age Group	*Trans Gomti*	*Old Lucknow*	*Malihabad*	*Total*
Yes	8 (13.79)	34 (16.83)	4 (4.85)	46 (12.64)
No	50 (86.21)	168 (83.17)	100 (96.15)	318 (87.36)
Total	58 (100.00)	202 (100.00)	104 (100.00)	364 (100.00)

Name of Vocational Training Centre	*Trans Gomti*	*Old Lucknow*	*Malihabad*	*Total*
Govt.	2 (14.29)	10 (71.43)	2 (14.29)	14 (30.43)
Private	6 (18.75)	24 (75.00)	2 (6.25)	32 (69.56)
Teaching	2 (33.33)	4 (66.67)		6 (13.04)
Computers	2 (8.33)	20 (83.33)	2 (8.33)	24 (52.17)
Tailoring	4 (25.00)	10 (62.50)	2 (12.50)	16 (37.78)

Vocational training among Muslim women has been reported negligible. It is also seen from Table 6 that only a small proportion of respondents i.e. 12.64 per cent was vocationally trained while majority of the respondents were not trained.

Higher education is the most crucial sector in the educational system of a country. In fact, this sector is the backbone of any industrial country. This sector not only develops human capabilities to a maximum extent possible but also empowers a person with knowledge, participation and ideas, which help him/her to contribute to the development process of the society more meaningfully and rationally. However, higher education remains still a far cry for majority of the people in India and more so with regard to women in higher education is found to be very low in the country. The percentage enrolment of women in this sector of total enrolment was 32.5 in 1991. Besides, during the last decades, the growth of women's enrolment in higher education has also been at a slow pace. In 1979-80, the per cent enrolment of women in higher education was 26.0, which increased marginally to 32.5 per cent in 1991. Moreover, in relative terms during the last decades the growth of enrollment of women in higher education was not steady.

TABLE 7

View Perception of Respondents Regarding Higher Education

Age Group	*Yes*	*No*	*Some Extent*	*Total*
Illiterate	16 (61.54)	6 (23.08)	4 (15.38)	26 (100.00)
Literate	56 (87.50)	6 (9.37)	2 (3.13)	64 (100.00)
Primary	12 (87.71)	2 (14.29)	—	14 (100.00)
J.H. School	26 (92.86)	2 (7.14)	-	28 (100.00)
High School	56 (100.00)	-	-	56 (100.00)
Inter	32 (94.12)	- (5.88)	2	34 (100.00)
Graduate	94 (97.92)	2 (2.08)	-	96 (100.00)
P.G.	46 (100.00)	-	-	46 (100.00)
Total	338 (92.86)	18 (4.94)	8 (2.20)	364 (100.00)

As far as the question of Muslim women, most of the respondents were in favour of higher education of their children (92.86 per cent) while meagre proportion of respondents i.e. 4.9 per cent were against higher education for their children. This was more pronounced in low educated and illiterate women as compared with highly educated respondents (Table 7).

Thus, it is clear that women are aware about the importance especially of higher education in the country in general and in the studied urban locate in particular. This awareness can be correlated with the overall educational level of the respondents. Their socio-cultural backgrounds like age, family structure, and education of father, husband, and the economic status of the family have shown direct relations of their educational level and also their views regarding different aspects of women's education. The respondents striving for further achievements through education, are quite clear from the views especially of the respondents with higher level of education. They want to receive job through acquiring higher education and make themselves economically independent. Majority of the respondents are also in favour of girls achieving higher education and most of them have ever opted for education institutions for educating their daughter or other girls in their family. Thus, the awareness towards achieving education and realizing its importance seems to be high in the respondents. They are of the opinion that education is the only means to change the traditional attitudes and values, which have lowered the status of women. It is that most of the Muslim women are aware about the importance of education. They agree that only education could enhance their social status.

REFERENCES

Hasan, Qumar (2000), "Life-Space Of Indian Muslims", *The Eastern Anthropologist,* Vol. 53, No. 3-4, Lucknow: Ethnographic & Folk Culture Society.

Hamid, Syed (1986), "Educational Status of Muslims", *Muslim India,* October.

Saxena, M.S. (1983), "Why Muslims don't fare well", *Times of India.* May, 31.

Shah, G. (1984), "The 1969 communal riots in Ahmadabad." In A. Ali Engineer (ed.) *Communal Riots in Post Independent India.* Hyderabad: Sangam Books.

PART – III

GENERAL

16

IDENTITY OF RELIGIOUS MINORITIES AND NATIONAL INTEGRATION IN INDIA

—Jag Mohan Singh Verma

Among the religious minorities in India, Muslims constitute the largest minority. It can also be said that they are the majority among the minorities, which consists of the followers of different religions namely Sikh, Christianity, Jain, Buddha etc. All these religious minorities had their distinct religious identities. Their identity makes a colourful religious pluralism in India and the national integration demands the registration of the participation of all those religious minorities groups in the mainstream of the national life. Religious minorities, in fact, are the most important component of national integration in India. Integration as just denotes a unified national life in several respects. It also stands for the national system of any country incorporating social, economic, educational, and cultural aspects. Logically integration is opposed to disintegration or the destabilizing forces in the national life of any country. Since integration is a positive concept, it is often recognized with a unified process of national lives and the integral identity of the country. However, integration has several dimensions linguistic, regional, religious, cultural, educational, political etc. still the unqualified use of the word integration often refers towards religious integration in a multiple plural society like India. Though linguistic and regional contours often become more pronounced than religious considerations. All in all religious integration alone which can broadly be supposed to incorporate social and cultural aspects as well.

Now the question arises whether a religion as much is a positive factor in integration or it acts as a dismantling force. It leads us immediately to look into the nation of religion. Religion, in general is defined as a belief or the worship of God but viewed from a broader angle religion refers to any thing to which one is totally devoted and which rules one's life. It means that religion provides a system of life. Since integration is an identity of a national life, it surely is a composition of the individual's lives. Religion also stands for moral and ethical values which are in a way the major underpinnings of social or national living. Going back in human history one would discover that before the evolution of the social livings, individualistic life styles did prevail among the human individuals. As a society grew into nations and countries came to have people devoted to several religions the problem of integration of national life come to be identified with religion and national integration. Religious teachings (of all religions) pertain to humanism, truth, sincerity, devotion and tolerance. But since religious inscription may be subjected to multiple interpret any religion in such a way as to fulfil their ulterior motives by emphasizing its negative aspects.

The problem of achieving national integration in modern India has been perhaps the greatest problem which we are facing today. National integration is a most important need for the survival and progress of free democratic Indian nation. The analysis of religion and national integration in India requires the description of religious and cultural history of India. But before we do so it would be in order to have a glance over the types of religions which are believed in and practiced in India. All the religions in India may be classified into four types from the viewpoint of their historical imprint on Indian society.

First, the primal Vernon of the pre-Aryan people of India—the Adivasis and Dalits. Second, Aryan Hinduism which came about five thousand years ago and became the dominant religion of India. Third, the Dravidian Hinduism which arose in the country to counter the oppressive tendencies of Aryan Hinduism because it was supposed to be an alien faith. Fourth, Indian Protestant religion such as Jainism, Buddhism and Sikhism which flourished over successive periods on Indian soil. Fifth, migrant religions which came to India through the immigrants of their followers such as Judaism, Zoroastrians, Bahais and sixth, religions which are believed to be the products of political conquest (Islam) or economic subjugation and colonialism (Christianity) over India. The incoming of Islam signifies political conquest and the colonization of the Indian economy by the British heralds the beginning of Christianity on a large scale in this country.

The first four of the above mentioned six categories are usually accepted as native religions of India and the religions of the last two categories (fifth and sixth) are dubbed as "alien" religions. Thus India became a multireligious country and it becomes pertinent to investigate the role of these religions in national integration of this country.

Along with religions, many races also came to India which made it a multi-racial country. We should remember that many races like Shak, Huns, Sithian and Mangols, etc.

came to India and made their varied kinds of contributions. India is an old society in the sense that it has a long history of about thousands of years in which many religions, races and culture met, intermingled and prospered. The history of this nation has been full of meeting of races, wars, invasions, coexistence and conflicts. Most of the major conflicts in the contemporary Indian nation have had their strong roots in its history.

Living with peace and struggling for existence are inherent in human nature. Therefore groups of persons within a religion and between religions often lived with peace and amity but occasionally stood up on conflict with each other. Whenever, conflict and tensions arose, these posed serious threats to integrated social and national life. Fortunately, India has a very long heritage and the religious conflicts, confrontations or subdued tensions occurred at certain intervals of time in the Indian history, the national life of the country got enough time to absorb in it those conflicts, tensions and rivalries which arose among various religions, races and communities from time to time. The long history of the country provided ample opportunity of absorption foreign religious influences and even conflicting influences of the native religions. This has been the main reason that the long historical background of the country could provide tolerance and produce an integrated national life over a period of time. It is important to mention that the long time span proved to be a great contributory factor in case of national integration in India. But as it is observed now so late in the day, in many East European countries or else where in the world, religious conflicts are occurring so fast and regularly that these countries are not able to absorb their shocks and the result is that the religious rivalries, ethnic armed conflicts and the emerging social tensions are denying the national integration in those countries. The religious conflicts, tensions and rivalries among various religious communities and the gulf between the masses and the classes re the main hurdles in national integration in many countries of the world. Many factors have been working at cross purposes to harm the realization of national integration in these countries . it is matter of serious concern that despite the United Nations resolutions, global efforts, and a plethora of human rights, many countries of the world find that the right kind of national integration is absent.

Now it is necessary to identify and discuss the causative factors that lead to religious conflicts in human society. It takes us to differentiate between the "soul" and "body" of a religion. While the soul or spirit of every religion exhibits no conflicts, whatever points of differences are observed, they emanate only from the body of the religion i.e. rituals associated with it. A glance over the record of religious or communal riots in India or else where would reveal that the basis of confrontation has been the observance of their rituals by their followers. This shows that the faith in any religion does not come in conflict with national integration, it is only the exhibition of the religious fervor which often creates problems. The possibility of religious conflicts and tensions increases more when there are many religions and many communities within a religion observing different rituals. It is also noteworthy that sometimes religious conflicts which disrupts national integration do not arise because of the observance of opposing rituals but the conflicts are thrust upon by petty politicians and vested interest groups who happen to back certain specific religions and communities. It is an open secret that religious animosity castism, fundamentalism, class differences, normlessness, blatant corruption and fissiparous tendencies have grown so much that those who value national integration are feeling shocked. However, the politics of the yester years, provided an opportunity in the form of freedom movement of the country in which the followers of all religions shedding away their religious identities joined in a unified manner and national fervor for winning the independence of the country from the foreign rule. Thus viewed the freedom movement of India provides a unique example of national integration in India. However, with independence of the country in 1947 the unfortunate partition of the country is often described as the regrettable religious culmination of events. But after the Independence with the adoption of the constitution once again a system of national living with a secular democracy came to stay in India. The constitution provisions for all citizens of the country, irrespective of their caste, creed, colour and religion offer an opportunity of an integrated national life.

Along with secular constitutional provisions and the beginning of planned social and economic development, an effort was made to provide yet another opportunity to all groups of persons—across religions, communities and religion—to participate in the process of development and become its equal beneficiaries. In modern India, it is the process of national integration because conflicts retard development and no religious group or community can afford to loose development and remain underdeveloped and therefore it is imperative for them to keep their chauvinistic religious overtones in the background and participate full-fledged in the process of development and integrated national living.

However, it may also be stressed that the physical or tangible process of social and economic development is not sufficient to usher in an era of stable national integration in India. The intangible aspects of national life are no less important. These elements may be expressed in terms of the attitudes of mind, and in this connection the following three aspects are noteworthy: (i) an attitude of mind which makes it natural and normal for every citizen to regard loyalty to the nation as being above group or sectional loyalties: (ii) an attitude of mind which makes it natural and normal for every group or section of the nation to subordinate its interests to national interests: and (iii) an attitude of mind which makes it natural and normal for the nation to think of the interests of every citizen and of every group and section of the nation.

In this way national integration would result not only from the process of physical development but also, which is perhaps more important, from the creation of the above mentioned intangible attitudes of mind. At the moment in India, these attitudes are largely absent. It is, therefore, necessary that these attitudes be inculcated among the people and the earlier the better for achieving a stable national integration in the country.

NOTES AND REFERENCES

1. Ahmad, A., (1960), *Studies in Islamic Culture in the Indian Environment*, Bombay, Oxford University Press.
2. Desai, A.R., (1981), *Social Background of Indian Nationalism*, Bombay, Popular Prakashan.
3. Dubois, A.J.A., (1897), *Hindu Manners, Customs and Ceremonies*, Oxford, Clarendon Press.
4. Dhawan, G.N., (1951), *Political Philosophy of Mahatma Gandhi*, Ahmedabad, Navjivan Publishing House.
5. Emerson, R., (1960), *From Empire to Nation*, Cambridge, Harvard University Press.
6. Guenon, R., (1945), *Introduction to the Study of Hindu Doctrines*, London, Luzac and Co.
7. Jaiswal, S., (1991), "Varna ideology and social change", *Social Scientist*, vol. 19, nos. 3-4, March–April.

8. Malik, S., (1979), *Social Integration of Scheduled Castes*, New Delhi, Abhinav Publications.
9. Mansergh, Nicholas (ed.), (1970), *Constitutional Relations Between Britain and India, The Transfer of Power*, Vol. 1 to 12, London, Her Majesty's Stationery Office.
10. Oommen, T.K., (1998), "Religion and Culture" in *Azad Academy Journal*, Lucknow, Vol. XIV, No. 8, Aug. 1-31.
11. Rao, B. Shiva, (1996), *The Making of India's Constitution, Selected Documents*, Volumes 1 to 4, New Delhi, Indian Institute of Public Administration.
12. Sekhar, Chandra (ed.), (1999), "National Integration: Its Essential Requisition", in *Young India*, New Delhi, Vol. 10, No. 9, October 9.
13. Shourine, Arun, (1997), *Worshipping False Gods*, New Delhi, Harper Collins Publications India Pvt. Ltd.
14. Singh, Tarlok, (1974), *India's Development Experience*, Delhi, Macmillan Co. of India.
15. Smith, A.D., (1971), *Theories of Nationalism*, London, Duckworth.
16. Thakur, L.D., (1985), "Gandhian Way to Integration", in L.D. Thakur and S.M. Sayeed (eds.), *The Art and Sciences of Politics*, Lucknow, Print House (India).
17. Verma, Jag Mohan Singh, (1991), *Democratic Ethos and Developmental Process in India*, New Delhi, Uppal Publications.
18. Weber, Max, (1968), *The Religion of India: The Sociology of Hinduism and Buddhism*, New York.
19. Weiner, M., (1966), *Modernisation: Dynamics of Growth*, New York, Basic Books.

17

MINORITY: CONCEPT AND STATUS

—*S.K. Singh*

The term 'minority' has been defined by the *Oxford Dictionary* as "the condition or fact of being smaller, inferior or subordinate" and also as "the smaller number or part of a number which is less than half of the whole number". By implication, therefore, a minority occupies a subordinate or inferior status as compared to that of a majority. The sociologist have defined 'minority' as "a group of people differentiated from others in the same society by Race, Nationality, Religion or Languag .... Further they lack relatively in power and hence or subjected to certain exclusions, discriminations and other differential treatments".

From the above mentioned definitions, the following main points emerge:

(i) Inferior or subordinate position of the minority *vis-a-vis* majority.

(ii) Minority is smaller in numerical strengths to majority.

(iii) Differentiation on the grounds of the Nationality, Religion, Race and Language from the majority.

(iv) Lack of power in the minority.

(v) Minority is subjected to exclusion, discrimination and differential treatment by the majority.

(vi) Group identification from within the minority itself.

(vii) Prejudiced attitude from the majority.

(viii) Self-segregation behaviour from within the minority.

(ix) Discrimination and exclusion behaviour from the majority.

All the above attributes necessarily need not be present in a group to be labelled as minority. Some times a single trait or a combination of it entitles a group to a minority status. Similarly there have been deviations also in the above traits. For instance the relative small strength of a social group to be known as a minority is not always mandatory. It may constitute more than 50% of the total population and yet be called a minority because of other differentiations like, culture, race, religion etc. e.g. Negroes who constituted the majority of population in Mississippi, Alabama and South Carolina were called a minority by the sociologists. Likewise Bantus constituting 80% of the population in South Africa were also termed as minority.

Differentiations: The main grounds for minorities to be differentiated according to the sociologists have been Nationality, Language, Race and Religion. A brief description of each of these is attempted as under.

(i) *National minority:* Its origin can be traced back to Europe, where it was applied to various nation groups inhabiting definite territories since long but have lost the sovereignty over it to more numerous people of other nationality. Sometimes the original inhabitants even dispersed to different locations to escape subjugation and exodus and thus became subordinate to the majority group enjoying the economic and political power. Those who stayed back were relegated to the second class citizenry and were made the object of exclusion and discrimination in respect of economic and political power by the dominant class.

(ii) *Language minority:* Differentiation based on language is best illustrated by India since times immemorial within two language stocks viz. Dravidian of South and Indo-Aryan of North. The differentiation of Dravidian into Tamil, Telugu, Malyalam, Kannada and a dozen others were not marked by definite historical events as was the case with differentiation of Latin into Italian, French, Spanish and Rumanian in the West. Physical boundaries of states in India were demarcated as nearly as possible to the language boundaries for administrative convenience. It is another matter that this differentiation on the basis of language has been over the years the constant factor of conflict and clash among various language minorities in the country. The great upsurge against Hindi language in the 1970s by the Southern states in particular amply illustrates this phenomenon.

(iii) *Racial minority:* Racial groups are differentiated by certain physical features inherited as a result of endogamy over a long period. Few races are considered pure biologically but this biological criterion is not always adhered to. On the basis of origin, the Aryan, Dravidians, Mangols, Chinese, Negroes etc. can be distinctly recognized. Even Whites and non-Whites in the U.S.A. have been the offshoots of a mixture of one or two races like Negroid or Mongoloids. Thus the minority on the basis of race does influence the societal moorings and has a great bonding effect which lasts.

(iv) *Religious minority:* Differentiation on the basis of religion is predominantly practised in the U.S.A. like Jews, Muslims, Christians, Eastern orthodox and Protestants. Religious minority status can be acquired voluntarily as against the nationality or racial status, which cannot be acquired as per wish. In India, there are religious minorities like Muslims, Christians, Sikhs, Parsis etc., who constitute quite a substantial percentage of population in the country.

The above differentiations present a substantive ground for a community to be recognized as minority but they need not remain consistent and even permanent. With the passage of time, the differentiation disappears as a consequence of assimilation, or other factors. This is the primary reason that a large number of minorities now are not heard of. Similarly new minorities emerge due to displacement of one national group from the parent nation on political grounds viz. Refugees in the different parts of the world.

Religious differentiation is still a prime source of minority status, although in Europe it has ceased to be so now. The most distinctive conflicts among religious minorities probably occurred after the Second World War viz. Hindu-Muslim in India and Muslims Jews in Palestine. Protestants have been subjected to discrimination in Catholic Spain and part of South America. Jews have been subjected most to discrimination in Soviet bloc countries in Europe. Religious minorities also include Christians in Muslim countries, Pagans and atheist in Christian countries, Hutterites and Donkhobors in Canada and minor religious groups like Sikhs and Parsis in Indian subcontinent.

Minorities and Society

Position of minority in a given society involves their assignment to a lower status in one or more of the following areas of life: (i) Economic (ii) political (iii) legal (iv) social.

To illustrate the above, a minority may be assigned a lower ranking occupation or lower compensated position within each occupation to deny its members the equal economic status in the society. Secondly it may be prevented from exercising full political rights and privileges held by the majority. Thirdly it may not be given equal status with majority in the application of law or justice and lastly it may be partially or completely excluded from formal as well as informal associations of the majority.

Quite frequently a minority voluntarily excludes itself partially or completely from participating in the above areas of life in the name of maintaining and preserving traditional cultural differences subordination by the majority and self-segregation of minorities usually accompanied the subjective attitudes of mutual hostility which are publicly denied by both majority and minority. Thus their relationships invariably, sometimes, implicitly and sometimes, explicitly involve certain degree of conflict which may take different shapes and levels.

Three types of hostilities or prejudices against the minority can be definitely discerned

(i) *Power:* the majority tends to exploit the minority for economic, political sexual and prestige purposes and the minority seeks to escape it with all the might at its command. The achievement of these by the majority may be brutal including enslavement of minority, but it is never personal and never results in the death of a minority person. The hostility based on power may be expressed in the form of exploitation like slavery, piracy, tribute, and suzerainty over political or military institutions of minorities, differential recommendations for work or even seizure of their women for sexual purposes. Human history is replete with all the examples in plenty e.g. Central Africa and South America present the good example of the power conflict.

(ii) *Ideology:* The majority believes that it has the monopoly on truth while the minority may also believe the same way. The ascendancy of majority in this respect may result in the conversion of the minority group to its version of truth. If resisted by the minority, the repercussion may be deadly e.g. exile or death. The accompanying social system of conflict with this hostility attitude is the caste system, which prohibits mobility across groups and attaining equal status. It also requires endogamy-systematized display off inferiority by the minority and occupational divisions of labour. It also has the pathological form which insists on physical extermination of minorities as it is believed to threaten the purity of the majority race. Racial conflicts have been most frequent in South Africa and U.S.A.

(iii) *Race:* The majority believes itself to be biologically superior to the minority and hence it stereotypes minority in terms of negative values and characteristics. The minority may have the same attitude towards majority. The conversion or extermination is the hostility attitude towards minorities on the basis off ideological differentiation. This is perhaps the most brutal and at the same time may be most generous towards the minority depending upon its attitude. Religious minorities of India and Palestine are the important example of this type. There have been quite a few examples of conversion of disadvantaged classes of majority Hindus to minorities Christians and Muslims. As a backlash of their mass conversion, brutal attacks (sometimes fatal) have been engineered by a few of the majority Hindus which have been decried by one and all. Recent enactment by Tamil Nadu to ban forced conversion or conversion by allurement is a state directed effort in this direction. Many more states are contemplating to enact some such law to put a brake on this practice.

Minority and Social Change

Generally, mere existence of a minority in a particular society is the constant stimuli, as well as irritant which provokes certain changes. Minority has a different culture from that of the majority. There has been a long-standing hypothesis that a contact and clash of cultures is the source of social change. Minority often breeds in a different deviant culture, even when it does not have a different culture to that of the majority. Further minorities are a source of social dissatisfaction and unrest, which are the necessary preconditions for social change. Minorities as a conflict group tend to upset the status quo. They require that the majority must readjust to them regularly which, if not done, results in clashes, sometimes brutal. They also form coalitions with other minorities to disrupt the balance of power in their favour. They often join reforms or revolutionary movements just to prove their worth as a compromise formula with the majority and to gain ascendancy in the dominant group.

The power consideration by the majority is maintained and here the minority provides the best example of social change. When power is not the consideration, the majority feels unconcerned about minority and allows it to have its own way. e.g. The dominant group may be busy in acquiring wealth and political power, the minority may engage itself in acquiring knowledge and skill which become the stimuli for social change in due course. Too much tolerance practised by the dominant group sometimes, results in their own destruction e.g. the famous historian Edwrard Gibbon has held this to be true about Romans and Christians in the later part of Roman Empire.

This has been held valid by a number of scholars, political leaders and others in case of Hindus and Muslims in India as well. They have voiced their sincere concerns about the policies followed by the successive governments at the centre and states which aimed at appeasing the Muslim minorities even at the cost of Hindus. They maintained that too much appeasement of the Muslims is not going to change their mindset towards Hindus and therefore they go against the majority. Gibbon's argument may not hold good completely in case of Indian Hindus, but too much tolerance is definitely costing the majority dearly internally as well as in its relations with neighboring state of Pakistan.

The minorities based on race or ideology tend to be not to create conditions conducive to social change but even they can bring a change in society in spheres not very prominent like, songs, humor, folktales etc.

II

MUSLIM MINORITIES IN INDIA

The secular Indian Constitution, though expressly forbidding discriminations on the basis of race, caste, religion, sex and place of birth etc., does practise it implicitly by providing specific safeguards to religious minorities. A special mention may be made here of the provisions under Article 29 and 30 where the religious minorities have been given differential treatment by the state. Similarly the provisions of other Articles under the Directive Principles of State Policy (Part II) also give preferential treatment to the minority groups. Further Part XIV of the Constitution gives preferential treatment to certain classes of people in the services of the union and states. Under Part XVI special provisions relating to certain classes of society have been given like S.C., S.T., Anglo-Indians in the representation to the Union parliament and state legislatures. But the framers of the Indian Constitution never considered the necessity of reservation of seats to religious minorities in the legislature and therefore did not provide for it in the Constitution. The granting special provisions to the minorities inevitably amounts to their differential treatment by the State which in term legitimizes the attitudes of the majority group towards them i.e. placing them in the subordinate or inferior position in the society. Thus, the State itself becomes the perpetrator of the differential treatment towards the religious minorities in placing them in a subordinate or inferior position in the society with all its good and well meaning intentions.

Minorities constitute 18% of the total population of the country as per 1991 census and the Muslim minority accounts for 12% of it. It is the largest second in the world only surpassed by Indonesia. The other minorities in the country account for just 6% of the total population together. Therefore, whenever issues concerning minorities are discussed at the government level, and plans and programmes are formulated and launched, only the Muslim minority, which is the majority among the minorities in the country, is always the target group. In fact minority term itself in common parlance has come to be understood and used for Muslim in India. The Muslims have been at the forefront of the national freedom struggle and there has been no dearth of them in any walk of life in the country. The government of India, beside the constitutional safeguards, has been earnestly trying to protect their interest by extending a number of benefits and facilities through multiple programmes and schemes over the years. A brief description of some of them has been attempted as follows to give a picture of State intervention for their growth, advancement and development.

The Ministry of Social Justice and Empowerment (previously known as Ministry of Welfare) has been charged with the responsibility of taking care of the minorities and other disadvantaged groups and communities in India. It has launched a number of programmes and schemes for their advancement and development in the fields of education and socio-economic upliftment. Maulana Azad Education Foundation was set up in 1989 by the Ministry as a voluntary, non-political, non-profit making social service autonomous organization to promote education amongst educationally backward sections of society, particularly the minority communities. The union government has been providing grants-in-aid to the institution under a planned scheme to build up a "Corpus Fund". Interest accrued thereon is utilised for pursuing the activities relating to educational advancement of minorities in the country. Rupees 2.85 crore has been released during 2000-2001. Since its inception, the foundation has sanctioned grants-in-aid amounting to Rs. 46.40 crores to 333 NGOs till December 2000.

The education base of minority students has been recognized as poor and calls for remedial coaching classes for middle and higher secondary level to enable them to compete with students of other social classes. Keeping in view this need, Remedial Coaching Scheme was started in 2000-2001 and Rs. 8.47200 were sanctioned to four NGOs to start coaching classes to minority students. The foundation also funded and financed the Lace Making Training cum production center at Pilibhit (UP) during 2000-2001 to help the minorities in skill building and production.

The Ministry has been operating the scheme of Pre-Examination Coaching for economically weaker sections of minorities and Backward classes to enable them to compete in the civil service and other exams for gainful employment. Since the beginning of the scheme in 1992-93, 27700 candidates have benefited through 380 institutions with a financial assistance of Rs. 1.80 crores till December 2000.

The Ministry of Home Affairs appointed a High Power Panel under Dr. Gopal Singh in 1980 which identified Muslims and neo Buddhists as educationally backward at the all India level. The National Policy of Education 1986 (updated in 1992) envisaged to pay greater attention to the education of educationally backward minorities to reap the fruits of equality and social justice. Accordingly, the Department of Secondary and Higher Secondary Education in the Ministry of HRD has started Educational Development programmes in minority concentrated areas. The Area

Intensive Programme for Educationally Backward Minorities is being implemented in 325 blocks of 13 states and three Union Territories beside in four districts of Assam to provide basic educational infrastructure and facilities. It is also implementing a scheme of modernizing Madarsa education which provides for assistance in teaching of Science, Maths, Social Studies and languages on a voluntary basis. A study carried out by Dr. Fahimuddin of the Giri Institute of Development Studies, Lucknow (2002) has come out with startling facts about modernizing Muslim Madarsas in U.P. It has found that grants made to teach Science, Maths and Social Studies by the Ministry of Social Justice and Empowerment. Government of India has not been utilised by Madarsas, neither they have shown any interest to take the advantage of the scheme. Since the scheme is voluntary one, the state efforts to assist Madarsas to modernize are negated by their unwillingness. Here the argument that the minorities tend to self-segregation hold true in the garb of maintaining their distinct identity as a social class.

Economic Development

National Minorities Development and Finance Corporation has been set up with authorized share capital of Rs. 500 crores to provide concessional finance to eligible minority people to set up a self-employment venture. The state governments and union territories contribute at prorata basis to this Corporation. It has financed 78995 beneficiaries with an amount of Rs. 274.41 crores till December 2000. The Corporation has also taken up the micro-financing through NGOs for helping out the poorest among the minorities, having no access to financial institutions. Till December 2000, beneficiaries numbering 2772 have got Rs. 11470 lakh under this scheme. Additionally, Rs. 27.62 lakh has been released to 41 reputed NGOs for formation of Self-help groups among the minorities.

To develop skill and entrepreneurship, the Corporation has organised several training programmes with special emphasis on traditional craftsmanship and occupation. Assistance is also provided by the Corporations to participate in the fairs and exhibitions to generate awareness amongst target groups. In 2000-2001 only, Social Development Fair at Pragati Maidan, New Delhi, Utsav by Hadoti Hast Shilp Sansthan of Rajasthan at Bangalore, Milan Mela by Minorities Development and Finance Corporation of West Bengal, at Calcutta were held to give support to small businessmen of minority to exhibit and sell their products.

The Corporation has sanctioned Rs. 21.60 lakhs in 2000-2001 to Annapurna Mahila Mandal for 400 women beneficiaries of minority communities in Mumbai under the micro-credit.

In pursuance of the strategy of area based approach to tackle the problems of minorities, the scheme of multi-sectional development plans was launched in 1995-96 in 41 minority concentrated districts. The scheme envisaged the concerned states to undertake surveys to prepare project reports through experts bodies in regard to activities conspicuously pursued by the minorities, with a view to identify the requirements of credit, marketing, training and technological support etc. for carrying out such activities in a viable way for their development and welfare in these districts. The central assistance is released to states for this purpose. Reports of 31 districts have been prepared and the state governments have been requested to implement the projects by pooling resources. The NMDFC has also been advised to prepare and implement schemes in these identified districts of minority concentration.

National Commission for Minorities Act was passed in May 1992 to give a statutory status to the Minorities

Commission making it a more effective body to safeguard the interest of the minorities under the constitutional provision. For the purpose of this Commission, the centre has notified five communities to be recognized as minorities viz.: Muslims, Christians, Sikhs, Buddhists and Zoroastrians. The Commission has submitted 8 reports so far which have been examined by various Ministries and Departments and follow up action is being taken. It has also set up a Minority Education Cell which exclusively looks after the problems of minority educational institutions regarding recognition, affiliation and grants-in-aid etc.

The Commission for Linguistic Minorities was established in July 1957 upon the recommendations of the State Reorganization Commission. It has its head quarters at Allahabad with regional offices at Kolkata, Belgaum and Madras. Rs. 81 lakh has been released in 2000-2001 to the Commission to pursue its statutory functions.

15 Point Programmes

These programmes for the welfare of the minorities may be classified in three broad categories, viz.

(i) Safety and protection of life and property.

(ii) Representation in jobs under central and state governments.

(iii) Social and educational development.

The programme is being implemented by the Central Ministries and Departments, State Governments and Union Territories. The Ministry of Social Justice and Empowerment obtains reports in respect of point 1 to 8 from the Ministry of Home Affairs. In respect of point 11 to 14 a half yearly report is obtained by the Ministry from the States and Union Territories. On the basis of the reports, the remedial measures are taken by the Ministry.

Ministry of Home Affairs has set up a Rapid Action Force charged with the special task of quelling the communal riots in any part of the country. Special guidelines to states have been issued for prevention of communal riots and for providing relief and rehabilitation to the riot victims. The guidelines for promotion of communal harmony issued in Act 1997 include enhancement of ex-gratia grant in case of death or permanent incapacitation. National Foundation for Communal Harmony set up under the Ministry of Home Affairs assists the children of riot victims and provides them educational and vocational training.

Departments of Personnel and Training has been given instructions to make it mandatory to all recruiting agencies to have at least one member belonging to minority on its selection Board where more than ten vacancies have to be filled in group C and D. Besides, Director General of Employment and Training, Ministry of Labour has also been instructed suitably. The AIR and Doordarshan is under obligation to further the minority development and take measures not to differentiate on minority ground only.

III

HUMAN DEVELOPMENT AMONG MUSLIMS IN INDIA

The best indicators of human development in a given community can only be adjudged and evaluated by the reports of the UNDP and India. While the UNDP reports do not give specifically the HDI in the religious groups, the India Human Development Report (1999) by the National Council of Applied Economic Research analyses the data, beside others, on the religious social group basis also. The multipurpose survey covered 33230 households in rural

India spread over 1765 villages of 195 districts in 16 states of the country including U.P. A great limitation with which the data suffers is that it concerns the rural population only while majority of the Muslims live in the urban conglomerations. Nevertheless, it does provide a definite lead to the status of HDI in the muslim minorities in the country. Taking a stock of the situation after state mounted efforts for advancement and development of the minorities in the country as discussed above it would not be out of place to ascertain the human development of the minorities on the basis of select indicators. An attempt has been made here to analyze the status of HDI among the minorities specially Muslims.

TABLE 1

Human Development Profile of Rural India

	Per Capita Income in Rs. Per Year	*BPL %*	*Proportion of Household Income spent on*	
			Health	*Education*
Hindus	4514	39	5.1	2.6
Muslims	3678	43	6.6	2.7
Christians	5920	27	5.7	3.1
Others	5427	34	5.3	3.5

Source: Compiled from the *India Human Development Report*, 1997.

Table 1 shows the Human Development Profile of rural India in 1994 where Hindus earned Rs. 4514/- per capita income per year while Muslims could earn Rs. 3678/- only which goes to prove the economic backwardness of both Muslims and Hindus in comparison to Christians, of course Muslims being at the bottom. Similarly 39% households in the sample of 33230 fall below poverty line (BPL) in the Hindus while 43% households of Muslim minority fall in this category which is 4% higher than

Hindu majority. Thus it goes to prove their poor economic status in the rural India in case of Christians only 27% households are bracketted under BPL category which depicts their better prosperity and economic status. Likewise percentage of household income spent on education and health varies among them. It stands at 2.6% and 5.1% on education and health among Hindus, 2.7% and 6.6% among Muslims and 3.1% and 5.7% among Christians respectively. This signify that the Christians are quite well aware about the benefits of good education and health and are able to expend on them more perhaps because of their better economic conditions as compared to Muslims and Hindus.

TABLE 2

Literacy Rates, Enrolment Rates and Matriculates among Religious Groups

	Literacy rate above 7 years			Enrolment Rates 6-14 years			Matriculated		
	Total	*Male*	*Female*	*Total*	*Male*	*Female*	*Total*	*Male*	*Female*
Hindus	53.3	65.9	34.2	72.0	78.1	65.1	8.5	12.0	4.7
Muslims	49.4	59.5	38.0	61.6	66.2	56.6	5.9	8.3	3.2
Christians	80.8	85.0	76.5	91.3	90.7	92.1	18.7	19.0	18.4
Others	53.8	62.9	43.8	78.5	83.2	73.6	11.5	15.3	7.3

Source: Compiled from the *India Human Development Report*, 1997.

Table 2 depicts the literacy rates (about 7 years group) and gender disparity among the religious groups. The Literacy percentage among the Hindus stood at 53.3% whereas it was 49.4% among Muslims and 80.8% among Christians. Similarly the percentage of literacy among the males was 65.9% and females 34.2% among Hindus, 59.5% (males) and 38.0% (females) among Muslims and 85% (males) and 76% (females) among the Christians. This signifies that the gender disparity is more pronounced among Muslims and Hindus. Likewise the enrolment rates (6.14 years) are much higher among the Hindus being 72% and lower (61.6%) among Muslim although they are still higher i.e., 91.3% among the Christians. A significant difference in the boys' and girls' enrolment is also witnessed correspondingly . If the percentage of students who have completed matriculation is taken into consideration, the gap among various religions groups seems widening. Among Hindus the percentage of matriculates was 8.5%, and among Muslims 5.9% and among Christians 18.7%. It was 12% males and 4.7% females among Hindus, 8.3% males and 3.2% females among Muslims and 19% males and 18.4% females among Christians. All this goes to prove that the educational development of Muslims is much less than Hindus and still less than Christians while both the minority communities get equal protection, safeguards and assistance from the State as discussed earlier.

TABLE 3

Fertility Rates and Use of Contraceptives (Married Women) among Religious Groups

	Fertility rates		*Use of Family Planning methods*	
	CBR per 100	*TFR (15-49 years)*	*EMV users (%)*	*Vasectomy, Copper T and Loop etc. (%)*
Hindus	32	4.2	36.3	37.6
Muslims	39	5.8	24.7	26.1
Christians	20	2.1	38.1	44.4
Others	28	3.9	46.7	41.5

Source: Compiled from the *India Human Development Report*, 1997.

Table 3 depicts the use of family planning methods and fertility rates, by different religious groups. The Child

Birth Rate (CBR) per 100 stands at 32, 39 and 20 among the Hindus, Muslims and Christians respectively which goes to prove their respective fertility in the reproductive age groups. Similarly the TFR (15-49 years) stands at 4.2%, 5.8% and 2.1% among Hindus, Muslims and Christians respectively which substantiates the above contention. The use of family planning methods by different religious groups does have a great bearing on the fertility of their women. The data gathered reveals that 36.3% among Hindus use EMW and 37.6% use other methods (Vasectomy, Copper T, Loop etc. among Muslims 24.7% and 26.1% and among Christians 38.1% and 44.4% respectively. This amply answers the high fertility rates among the Muslims which is much less than the Hindus and the reasons for this comparatively small percentage among Muslims using family planning methods have not been documented by the report. Yet, there is a common perception among general public that Muslims normally do not believe in family planning, beside economic compulsions which squarely apply to other religious groups. Some say that their religions moorings do not permit them to interfere in the god ordained reproduction process while others observe that their non acceptance of family planning is the considered belief to augment their numerical strength to overcome the differentiation and exclusion by the Hindu majority.

Table 4 shows average annual income by source among different religious groups. In the agriculture and allied activity, the Hindus get Rs. 20828/- per capita per year while Muslims receive only Rs. 16388/-. The Christians receive the compensation at par with Hindus. In the artisans and individual work category the Christians top the list with 13336/- followed by Muslims with Rs. 12260/- and Hindus Rs. 10806/- only. This goes to prove the popular perception that the Muslims are better self employed and good artisans. In the Organised trade and business, Muslims do better than Hindus and the Christians falls far behind the two. In the qualified professionals category also Muslims fare better with an average of Rs. 17444/- as against Hindus with Rs. 15965/-. Similarly in the non-agricultural wages, they also get better remuneration than their Hindu counterparts.

TABLE 4

Distribution of the Religious Group Households Income-wise

	Agriculture and Allied Activity	*Artisans and Industrial Worker*	*Organised Trade or Business*	*Qualified Profess-ionals*	*Non Agricul-tural wages*
Hindus	56.1 (20828/-)	4.3	1.8	0.5	6.2
Muslims	44.1 (16388/-)	8.3	2.9	0.8	7.4
Christians	46.3 (20697/-)	2.9	1.9	8.4	7.8
Others	60.3 (30315/-)	3.1	0.6	0.8	5.0

Source: Compiled from the *India Human Development Report*, 1997.

Accordingly to the National Sample Survey Organisation (an autonomous institution under the Ministry of Statistics and Programme Implementation, Government of India) which submitted its 55th report on the basis of survey conducted in 1999-2000, the Muslims suffer from greater economic deprivation than Hindus. This is more so in urban India where a larger portion of their population resides. A larger portion of Muslims suffer from low level of expenditure on consumption i.e. on food, clothing, entertainment and others. The average expenditure by each member of a family was less than Rs. 300/- per month in 29% of rural Muslims while it was only 26% among Hindus (among the bottom 20% of the rural population).

This difference is much less in urban areas where about 40% Muslims fall in this category as against mere 22% Hindus correspondingly among the top 20% of the Hindus and Muslims as per consumption expenditure. Their percentage was 12% and 14% in rural areas and 6% and 17% in urban areas. This proves amply their respective economic status and power to spend an essential items which are the indicators of H.D.I., Further, the Muslim households having access to land in rural areas, 51% cultivate very little land, while this percentage is less in Hindus. To make matters worse for Muslims in terms of economic status, in the urban areas, only 27% households had a member on the regular salaried job as against 43% among Hindus. The unemployment among Muslims is higher than Hindus in rural areas which stood at 2.1% and 1.4% and in urban areas at 5% and 4.7% respectively.

The education levels also was much lower among Muslims. Only 48% among them (above 7 years) could not read and write as against 44% among Hindus in rural areas. This gap was wider in the urban areas i.e. 30% Muslims and only 19% Hindus fall in these categories. Thus Muslims minorities have done more poorly than their Hindu majority in respect of expenditure on consumption on education, employment and land holding. The changes due to growth and development on account of State interventions do not indicate that the gap between the two is closing in. This is very clear from the Table No. 5 given below.

TABLE 5

Percentage of Population in Bottom 20% Accordingly to Monthly Consumption Expenditure

(As Percentage of Population in Each Religious Group)

	Hindus	*Muslims*	*All Religions*
Rural			
1993-94	19	20	19
1999-2000	26	29	26
Urban			
1993-94	17	30	19
1999-2000	22	40	25

Source: Compiled from *National Sample Survey Organisation Reports* no. 438 and 468.

It is depicted that the bottom 20% of the households according to the level of consumption in both the communities in 1993-94 was: Hindus 19%, Muslims 20% in rural areas and 17% and 30% in urban areas respectively. This percentage increased in 1999-2000 to 26% and 29% in the rural areas and 22% and 40% in the urban areas. This illustrates that the gap between the two main religious groups has not been closing in, instead it is increasing. It was only 11% in 1993-94 in rural areas and 13% in urban areas which came down to only 3% in rural areas and increased to 18% in the urban areas. The causes of this phenomenon have to be researched thoroughly and the policy initiatives taken accordingly.

To sum up, the Muslims in India have been at crossroads since Independence. Inspite of Constitutional safeguards and a plethora of programmes and schemes launched for their upliftment, they remain at the lower level of scale in almost all walks of life, exceptions notwithstanding. This status has to be studied in the context of the attributes of a minority given in the part I of this paper. Their growth prospects in all fields surely depend on their own mindset, self-efforts, willingness and earnest desire to be assimilated in the mainstream of the nation. However this will not give desired results until and unless the majority Hindus also do not welcome them with open arms discarding and disbanding the age old prejudices and exclusions. Besides, international and bilateral relations do have to be worked out in tandem to propagate the external Indian philosophy of universal brotherhood, peace and happiness.

REFERENCES

1. Abusaleh Shariff Arnold M. Rose *Encyclopedia of Social Sciences.*
2. C. Rammanohar Reddy, *The Hindu,* New Delhi 12,13 September 2002.
3. Constitution of India, Bare Act.
4. Government of India, Ministry of Social Justice and Empowerment, *Annual Report,* 2000-2001.
5. Government of India, Ministry of Finance, *Economic Survey 2001-2002.*
6. Hasan, Mushirul, *Legacy of A divided Nation: India's Muslims Since Independence,* Oxford University Press, New Delhi, 1997.
7. *India Human Development Report.*
8. Joseph Mathew, *Contemporary Religious Conversions,* Authors Press, New Delhi, 2001.
9. Laura D. Jenkins, *"Caste, Class and Islam: Boundaries of Backwardness in India," Eastern Anthroplogist,* Lucknow, Volume 53, No. 3, 4, 2000.
10. Nadeem Hussain, "Religion and Society Among Shias," *Eastern Anthroplogist,* Lucknow, Volume 53, No. 3, 4, 2000.
11. National Council for Applied Economic Research, Delhi 1997.
12. National Sample Survey Organisation, Government of India, New Delhi, Report No. 438 and 468.
13. *Oxford Dictionary.*
14. Quamar Hasan, Life Span of Indian Muslims, *Eastern Anthroplogist,* Lucknow, Volume 53, No. 3, 4, 2000.

18

NATIONAL COMMISSION FOR MINORITIES WITH SPECIAL REFERENCE TO MUSLIMS

—Kamal Srivastava

In Social Sciences in India a question that has been generally evaded is: in what terms to define the 'minority'. Neither Constitution of India, nor the Judiciary which is the interpreter of the Constitution, has defined the minority in precise terms. The Minorities Commission did not define minority too. Contemporary Sociologists generally define a minority as a group of people—differentiated from others in the same society by race, nationality, religion and language—who both think of themselves as a differentiated group with negative connotations. Further, they are relatively lacking in power and hence are subjected to certain exclusions, discriminations and other differential treatment. The important elements in this definition are a set of attitudes – those of group identification from within the group and those of prejudice from without – and a set of behaviors — those of self-segregation from within the group and those of discrimination and extension from without.

A minority need not to be traditional group with a long-standing group identification. It can arise as a result of changing social definitions in a process of economic or political differentiation.

The increasing saliency of a certain occupation, for example, can set apart the people who practise the occupation, if occupation more or less hereditary in the society and cause them to be considered a minority group. Language or religious variations in a society is considered unimportant for thousands of years, but a series of political events sharpen the religious or linguistic distinctions that the followers of one variation who happen to be without much power in the society are thereafter considered a minority.

The majority—minority has been an issue before our nation since the dawn of Independence. The British rulers posed themselves as the sole protector of the minorities in India. That led to the Hindu-Muslim divide and partition of the nation. The Muslim League stood up as the sole guarantor of the rights and safety of the Muslim minority.

The Government of 'Independent India' for the sake of a united, integrated nation, stood for the protection of the interests of the minorities in India. Since then, the minority continued to remain a political question frequently raised and debated for political use.

Who are the minorities? What do they want? What is their need? The majority vis-à-vis the minority – these issues continued to bother the academics, the policy makers, and the political leaders of India.

Since the late sixties, the minority question became sharper and more glaring when Mrs. Indira Gandhi set up a governmental machinery to look into the special problems of the minorities as a step towards promoting national integration. That the minorities mentioned by Mrs. Gandhi implied the Muslim of India becomes more or less clear from her reference to Urdu, and particularly to her desire to see that the Urdu was assured its Constitutional guarantee. Since then, the minority question became more pronounced; socio-economic, educational backwardness continued to persist.

Mrs. Gandhi's attitude to Muslim demands, her inclination towards the Muslim communal organizations, her handling of Urdu aggrandizing demand, led to the minority being politically exploited.

The Muslim League always asserted that "it was the custodian of the interests of the Muslim minority in India". It is an irony that the Muslim League in Kerala passed a resolution demanding due recognition for Urdu even though the Kerala Muslims speak Malayalam.

Thus, the minority question became more crucial in India since 1967 general election and can be largely attributed to the propaganda carried out during the poll campaign (1967).

The concept of minority in India continued to remain the game of power, played by the political parties / groups or State to reorient the belief and motivation of that particular group.

To define a minority as a social category, in a given society, who, because of their distinct physical or cultural characteristics, find themselves in situations of inequality within that society. A minority may be further defined as a group which is perceived as such by the other groups.

Minorities, as derived from the Constitution of India, include the Buddhists, the Christians, the Muslims, the Parsis, and the Sikhs, but, in common parlance, the term is generally understood to be equated with the Muslims. The Jains and the Bahais do not find any mention.

Minority in India has become a political term, with a political tinge; the minorities have been politically used, but their real problems of educational backwardness remain. The minorities have been used for the purpose of garnering votes after Independence, but their socio-economic, educational problems have remained unattended.

The word minority as stated earlier has not been defined in the Constitution. The full Bench of the Kerala High Court 1964 (2) Ker. 478 (F.B.) held that as the word minority has not been defined in the Constitution, any community, religious or linguistic, which was numerically less than 50 per cent of the population of the state was a minority, and thus was entitled to the protection of Article 30. The Bench thus found that the Roman Catholics were a minority in Kerala.

Further the Apex Court summarized the effect of the decision in Sidharajbhai's case in the following propositions:

(i) "A school established by a minority—whether before or after the Constitution is within the ambit of Article 30(I), even though it imparts general education....";

(ii) The right guaranteed by Article 30(I) is a right that is absolute, and any law or executive direction which infringes the substance of that right is void to the extent of the infringement;

(iii) The absolute character of the right does not preclude regulations in the true interests of efficiency of instruction, discipline, health, sanitation, morality, public order and the like, as such regulations are not restrictions on the substance of the right guaranteed by the Constitution;

(iv) The fundamental right enshrined in Article 30(I) (Cultural and Educational Right) is intended to be effective and should not be whittled down by any regulative measure conceived in the interest, not of the minority educational institution, but of the public or the nation as a whole.

There are divergent views on the minority-majority question in India. An Indian Journalist Myron Weiner quotes to India as a "Hindu island in an Islamic sea." The Government of India has notified five communities namely Muslims, Sikhs, Christians, Buddhist, Jains and Zoroastrians as minorities at the National level. Apart from Zoroastrians which has negligible number than other communities has been depicted in the following table.

(in percentage)

Population by Religion	*1961*	*1971*	*1981*	*1991*
Hindus	83.5	82.7	82.6	82.4
Muslims	10.7	11.2	11.4	11.7
Christians	2.4	2.6	2.4	2.3
Sikhs	1.8	1.9	2.0	1.9
Buddhists	0.7	0.7	0.48	0.77
Jains	—	0.47	—	0.41

The Muslims have steadily increased from 10.7% of the total population in 1961 to 11.2% in 1971 to 11.4% in 1981 and to 11.6% in 1991. The Christian population is slightly on decline. The population of the Sikhs, Jains and Buddhists remains almost the same. The increase in population among the Muslims is on account of two factors, i.e., natural growth of population, that is increased birth rate, and immigration from neighbouring countries particularly, Bangladesh.

To evaluate the working of various safeguards in the Constitution for the protection of religious minorities and to make recommendations to ensure effective implementation and enforcement of all the safeguards and laws, a Minorities Commission was set up in January 1978. The Minorities Commission was constituted by a Resolution of Government of India No. II-16012/2/77 NID (D) dated January 12, 1978 issued by the Ministry of Home Affairs (later on amended in Ministry of Welfare Resolution No. IV 14011/2/38-CLM dated March 30, 1988) to monitor working of the safeguards provided in the Constitution and Laws enacted by Parliament and the State Legislature. It had the following principal mandates:

To evaluate working of various Constitutional safeguards for protection of minorities as well as for safeguards enshrined in laws; to make recommendations for effective implementation of such safeguards and laws; to undertake a review of the implementation of the policies in regard to minorities pursued by the Union and State Governments; to suggest appropriate legal and welfare measures in respect of any minority to be undertaken by Central and State Governments; to look into specific complaints regarding deprivation of rights and safeguards of minorities; and to serve as a National Clearing House of information in respect of condition of the minorities.

After enactment by Parliament of the National Commission for Minorities Act 1992 (19 of the 1992) the Government of India in their Notification So No. 317(E) dated 17.5.1993 issued by Ministry of Welfare have reconstituted the Commission with effect from 17.5.1993.

On above perspective how far the National Commission for Minorities has attained the objectives like; communal harmony, employment avenues, educational and socio-economic development.

Communal Harmony

In the wake of Ayodhya incident on December 6, 1992, the Members of the Commission visited the riot affected areas and the Commission requested the State Governments of Uttar Pradesh, Assam, Andhra Pradesh, Gujarat, Haryana, Karnataka, Madhya Pradesh, Maharashtra, Rajasthan and West Bengal to send reports on the following aspects.

(i) Compensation actually disbursed to the affected persons – Number of cases and amount.

(ii) Financial assistance extended by Banks and Insurance Companies to the riot affected people bank wise and according to location giving the number of applicants. Claims filed, number of cases rejected and reasons for each rejection, number of cases under process, number of cases yet to be taken up.

On above guidelines, the Minorities Commission recommended the ex-gratia for the tragic loss of human lives Rs. 2 lakhs. The Commission has been regularly monitoring the progress in the disbursement of relief and rehabilitation to the victims with the concerned State Governments and Reserve Bank of India.

State Minorities Commission of Uttar Pradesh has organised a conference for National Communal Harmony at Lucknow with the help of Government of India.

The participants of conference were eminent and learned Muslims, Christians Methodist and Catholic Church,

Ambedkar Maha Sabha and Hindus from different parts of States. The focus of the Conference was 'Live and let live' of social agenda. A resolution was passed to spread out above said theme in the whole State.

EDUCATION AND EMPLOYMENT AVENUES

There has been no comprehensive survey on the issue of employment of Minorities. Gopal Singh Panel observed from sample data collected from different offices in different districts of the country (mostly pertaining to Income Tax, Customs and Central Excise, Offices of the Accountants, General etc.), the percentage of employment in Central Government Offices was 4.41% of the total population. The National Policy of Education 1986 (updated in 1992) envisages paying greater attention to the education of the educationally backward Muslims in the interest of equality and social justice. The Department of Secondary and Higher Secondary Education, Ministry of Human Resource Development, has started programmes of educational development.

Scheme for modernization of Madarsa Education under which financial assistance is provided for teaching of Science, Mathematics, Social Studies and Languages in traditional educational institutions (Madarsas/Maktabs). In Uttar Pradesh 735 Madarsas/Maktabs are running where 12 Madarsas are situated in Uttaranchal now. In the process of modernization the above mentioned subjects are being taught with the different teachers. The salaries of teachers are distributed by the grant which is Rs. 3,000/- per month.

Maulana Azad Education Foundation has been set up as an autonomous organisation with the objective of promoting education amongst educationally backward sections of Muslim society. The Central Government has been providing grant-in-aid to the Foundation under a plan scheme for building up a 'Corpus Fund'. Rs. 2.85 crore was released as a grant to the Foundation during 2000-2001.

Education is the most serious and conspicuous area of Muslim Minorities. The Muslim Communities are lagging behind in the field of education and do not have adequate opportunities to provide modern education to their children. At the instance of Minorities Commission the UGC in 1984 had formulated a scheme of coaching classes for competitive examinations for minority communities in certain Universities, Colleges in the country. It has been stated in the Programme of Action, New Education Policy 1986, that Muslims are educationally backward minorities. Since inception of the Scheme in 1992-93 to 31.12.2000, 27,770 candidates have been benefited from the Scheme through financial assistance provided to 380 institutions (NGOs) for various competitive examinations. The expenditure under this scheme was Rs. 3.65 crore during 8th Five Year Plan. During 2000-2001, against a provision of Rs. 2.50 crore, a sum of Rs. 1.80 crore has been released under this scheme up to December 2000. While the problems of literacy and unemployment affect the minority publication in general, the worst sufferers are the minority women, especially their Muslim counterparts. Their work participation rate and consequent contribution to the household income is abysmally low. For the education purpose the U.P. Government has taken initiative to construct exclusive Girl's Hostel in thickly Muslim areas. Till 1997-98, 5 hostels were constructed in Lucknow, Bareilly, Moradabad, Bulandshahr and Amroha respectively. Two new hostels were proposed in Pilibhit and Sidhartha Nagar districts in 1998-99 along with School buildings.

SOCIO-ECONOMIC DEVELOPMENT

The problem of economic backwardness is directly linked to the educational backwardness which renders them less equipped for gainful employment or for availing of self-employment opportunities. Right from the beginning, the high dropout rate of school children results in their lower representation in public employment and distinctively lower availment of socio-economic benefits of development programmes. The Commission lays great stress on the economic development and measures for this purpose. As long as they remain economically backward, their social condition would not improve and they would not be able to make any useful contribution to national development. It was, therefore, considered necessary to take various steps to improve their economic condition and to step up their economic progress. In this connection, the Commission wishes to emphasise the important role that could be played by Banks and Financial Institutions.

The National Minorities Development & Finance Corporation (NMDFC) has been set up with an authorized Share Capital of Rs. 500 crore for providing concessional finance to eligible beneficiaries belonging to minorities for setting up self-employment ventures. Government of India's share in the equity of NMDFC is subject to prorata contribution from the State Government / UT Administration. The Corporation has paid-up share capital of Rs. 212,12 crore, out of which Central Government has contributed Rs. 177 crore and States / UTs have paid Rs. 35.12 crore. Till December 2000, NMDFC has financed 78,995 beneficiaries involving an amount of Rs. 272.41 crores. NMDFC has taken up micro financing through NGOs for assisting the poorest among the minorities, who have no access to financial institutions. Under the scheme, till December 2000, Rs. 114.70 lakh has been disbursed to 2,772 beneficiaries. Besides, Rs. 27.62 lakh has been provided as interest free loan for formation of Self Help Groups through 41 reputed NGOs.

With a view to develop skills and entrepreneurship, NMDFC has organized training programmes with particular stress on the craftsmen engaged in traditional occupations and trades. Assistance is also provided for participation in exhibitions and fairs etc. to generate awareness amongst the target group about the prevailing market demand. NMDFC sponsored beneficiaries for participation in the Social Development Fair 2000 organized at Pragati Maidan from 15-21 May, 2000 amongst special measures taken during the year for benefit of craft persons who constitute a significant section of targeted beneficiaries, were released grant-in-aid for design/product development in Naga crafts to Lovely Multipurpose Cooperative Society. This is expected to help promote its domestic as well as export sides. A 10 day long exhibition cum sale called 'Utsav' was organized by Hadoti Hastshilp Sansthan from Rajasthan at Bangolore in September, 1999. With support from NMDFC 'Milan Mela 2000' was held by the West Bengal Minorities Development and Finance Corporation at Calcutta for supporting small business owners to exhibit their products.

The National Minorities Development and Finance Corporation, under the aegis of the Ministry has sanctioned Micro Credit of Rs. 21.60 lakh to Annapurna Mahila Mandal for 400 women beneficiaries belonging to minorities in Mumbai. The NGO is gearing up to increase the coverage under NMDFC scheme in other parts of Maharashtra, Karnataka and Goa in a phased manner.

It has to be well understood that India has variegated and yet, essentially unified culture in which all have shared substantially. Jawaharlal Nehru (in his convocation address in Aligarh Muslim University in 1948) said "You are Muslim and I am a Hindu. We may adhere to any religion, faith or even to none; but that does not take away from that cultural inheritance that is yours as well as mine. The past holds together, why should the present or the future divide us in spirit?"

People may have different faiths, beliefs, forms of worships, customs and manners. Yet they may be held together by a common band of cultural heritage which India acquired from antiquity. The irritants between the minorities and majority may be dissolved by creating a bond of India's citizenship with common heritage to share, and equality of rights and opportunity to enjoy. The socio-economic, educational problems of the minorities must be meticulously attended to Education which is the key to social and economic progress.

REFERENCES

State Minorities Commission, Uttar Pradesh, *Samvad Patrika.*

Annual Report 2000-2001, Ministry of Social Justice and Empowerment, Government of India.

Selected Works of Jawaharlal Nehru, Second Series, pp. 24-25.

R.N. Thakur, *Minorities: Towards a Conceptual Clarification.*

G.S. Ghurye, *Whither India* pp. 401-02, 407, Papular Prakashan, Mumbai, 1974.

19

MUSLIMS VS. HINDUS: EDUCATION AS THE GREATER LEVELER

—*Amitabh Thakur*

India is a country, which can boast of being the home of two of the most important religions of the world-Hinduism and Islam. Islam came to India almost immediately after it was formalized by Prophet Mohammed in Arabia in the seventh Century. By the beginning of the eighth century it had reached Sind though its area of influence remained limited for the next three centuries when it finally came to stay in India with the arrival larger part of India. The Muslim rulers, be it the various dynasties of Delhi or Agra including the Great Moghul and the lesser empires spread all over the country did help in establishing and strengthening this rather new religion in various parts of India. But it was much because of the effects and influence of the various Sufi saint and other proselytizers. Over a period of time the population of Muslims in this country increased in a big way, so much so that today it has more Muslims than any country in the world except a few.

Though the emergence of a newer kind of people who practised a totally different religion and at times held radically opposite views on so Civilization, what has generally been termed as a *Composite Culture* and a synthesis but the fact remains that unlike each of the earlier people who had come to India to subsequently lose their individual identities after having got assimilated into this great cultural cauldron with amazing ability to get other cultures sucked into its own, Islam remained distinct and it could retain its individuality and characteristic distinction. It remains true even today and despite having undergone long periods of British rule during which both Hindus and Muslims felt as much of being slaves to the foreigners as the other party and had at times come together to throw the foreign yoke but ultimately the distrust and the differences proved too greater for them to come together. The result was only the bifurcation of the nation but also permanent cleavage between the two religious groups, which persists even today.

The differences and the distances apart, what still remains a seminal problem and one, which makes things still worse, is the fact that the two communities have not become compatible economically and financially. While both these religious groups have their share of rich people along with those who are leading life of abject poverty. Yet unlike the Muslims who seem to have withdrawn themselves more and more into shell of their own resulting in what can be called a ghetto civilization, the Hindus have come to occupy the Centre stage in all the spheres of life including the Social, Economic, Political and Cultural. In fact even the literacy rate among the Muslims is much below the average literacy rate that prevails among Hindus which has resulted into more and more Hindus having gone into Government and Private Sector services as compared to their Muslim counterparts. This has made possible the emergence of a strong and vocal middle intelligentsia class among the Hindus, which seems to be lacking among the Muslims. The rise of the middle class has acted as a catalyst for further growth and shaking of the priestly regime with consciousness and modern ideas slowly but definitely percolating, this cannot be said to be true of the Muslims majority of who still remain in the strong grips of their clergymen who still extol the ancient and worn out ideas and values.

This is the classic vicious circle, which we talk about so often when dealing with the developing countries, which grow poorer, and the developed countries on the other hand go on becoming richer and richer, something of the same kind has happened in India in between the Hindus and the Muslims. The cultural and the socioreligious differences seem to be reinforcing the economic conditions and they feed and strengthen each other. If this vicious circle has to be broken it is quite imperative and absolutely essential that a multi-pronged strategy has to be devised which will act simultaneously at different front.

The fundamental requirement is literacy and education. As has been seen so clearly in Kerala if the people get properly educated rest of the things automatically start following. All the other indices of life, which denote the betterment of living conditions, are greatly dependent on education and literacy rates. Once the literacy rate increases, there will be corresponding and proportionate decrease in the rate of population growth, one of the most controversial ideas in India regarding Muslims. While it might be a matter of research and interpretation whether Islam allows for family planning or not but the fact remains that among educated Muslims one hardly finds a family having more than two to three children. So it seems this remains valid only where there is lack of education.

There are other related issues, some of which tend to generate much heat without any reason. Because of centuries of mutual distrust and distancing bordering to animosity, the two groups have not much love lost. The result is that anything that is said by one group is treated with contempt and vehemence by the other. More often that not the other group concludes that the suggestions made and the solutions provided are more because of some ulterior and mischievous motive.

What is the way out? To me it seems to be nothing other than education. Education and knowledge is a great path breaker. It is not than an educated man becomes the best human being and losses all his vices and gets rid of all his shortcomings but then he certainly tends to behave differently and more suavely than his uneducated counterparts. The sense of rationality and logic also seems to permeate in his mind. Hence an educated person has a better chance of judging things on their merits instead of getting swayed away be rhetoric, jingoes and absurdities. He knows and can make a better judgement regarding what is good for him and his family and their respective advancements and betterments.

Education as the core of development and the chief facilitator of the socioeconomic progress that is desired among the Muslim community is what I would like to dwell upon in my thesis. It can easily be seen that one of the primary reasons for the economic and the accompanied socio-cultural backwardness of the Muslim community is the lack of spread of education in the correct perspective and in the required amount.

But it is easier said than done. Moreover this kind of oversimplification is fraught with many inbuilt dangers as well and at times might prove to be quite misleading. Hence I propose to look into the question of education in coordination and along with the other important parameters.

Only after having taken a holistic view, keeping in the centre education and its effects, can we be able to arrive at the logical and correct perspective. In addition we must also look into the kinds of education that a very large section of the Muslim community is currently undertaking and the effects thereof on their overall development and also in deciding the future of the country. Whether such an education is justified and is to be encouraged or it should be curbed with a strong hand or otherwise is to be followed in a limited way is what the policy makers and education-administrators of this country must think about with deep concern.

Having given the outline of my the socio-economic scenario of the Muslims in this country along with the educational and literacy picture of this section. I think I have been able to bring out before you the realm of my sub-theme which firmly believes that mass scale modern education of the liberal school with emphasis on the concepts of freedom, equality and liberty is what will act as the correct anecdote for the Muslim society in getting rid of its socio-economic backwardness.

ANNEXURE

RECOMMENDATIONS OF THE NATIONAL SEMINAR ON MUSLIM MINORITIES IN INDIA: THE GROWTH PERSPECTIVE*

The Seminar which was inaugurated by Hon'ble Justice H.N. Tilhari, Chairman U.P. Backward Classes Commission, discussed threadbare the growth perspective of Indian Muslims who are the second largest community in the country. The issues like socio-economic development, education, population and health and empowerment of women were the highlight of the discussions during the two-day deliberations. Nearly 30 papers were contributed by various authors who hailed from various strata of society like academicians, bureaucrats, social workers and even retd. Military officers.

Recommendations of the Seminar

General Observation: The participants were of the view that there is a little difference between majority or minority communities living in rural areas in the matters of literacy, poverty, employment, health and nutritional care and the like. However, there is much difference in urban areas which need immediate attention to the problems. The recommendations are divided into three broad categories: education, economic status and growth and empowerment of women.

1. Education

The universalization of elementary education has remained an elusive dream and is even more dismal amongst the educationally backward communities like Muslims. In order to cover up the gap the following recommendations

---

* Organised by: Institute for Applied Research and Development, Lucknow.

are made:

There is a need to modernize the traditional institutions serving the Muslim community, for this:

(a) The 30,000 'Maktabs' in U.P., where teaching is limited to the reading of holy 'Quran' and little bit of Urdu be converted into non-formal education centres by providing another local teacher to teach Hindi, elementary Maths, and English. After completion of non-formal education, a child can join the regular stream through admission to the sixth standard in government or government aided schools. Bangladesh have already made an experiment to modernize 'Maktab' education with help of UNICEF. This step will help in immediate opening of 30,000 primary schools for Muslims overnight in U.P. alone. The experiment can be extended in other states also.

(b) There are 2,000 Arabic-Persian 'Madarsas' in U.P. alone where students spend up to 16 years on studies. Presently these institutions are teaching only Muslim theology. There have been experiments in Bihar and West Bangal to modernize these 'Madarsas' so as to include modern education together with the study of religion. This experiment can be replicated in other states. Such a step will mean opinion of 2,000 Intermediate colleges in U.P. alone which may be in the times to come be converted into even a degree or post-graduate college.

(c) In the field of technical and medical education the Muslims are far behind in spite of various incentive schemes like coaching, loans etc. It is better to allow the Muslim organization of credibility to open technical/medical colleges, but even this will not solve the problem as admission to these institutions have to be done only on merit or payment of heavy donation. But if the status of minority institutions is accorded to them 50% Muslim boys/girls can be admitted to these institutions.

(d) Another area is to provide vocational training to the Muslim, as they happen to be good artisans, mechanics, tailors, carpenters, electricians and so on. There are enough funds in IRDP (TRYSEM) & NRY for the purpose. However, if the period of training is extended to six months or one year in certain vocations then there may an enormous growth in their income, as there is a possibility of a tailor becoming a fashion designer.

(e) Minorities being otherwise lagging behind in terms of Human Development Index, the socio-economic conditions of women and girls is bound to be worse. To make tangible dent, a special dispensation will have to be made. It is recommended that Muslims be encouraged to open at least one girls high school in the private sector in each Muslims concentration block and one inter-college for girls at all the districts headquarters wherein other communities can also avail the facility.

2. *Economic Status and Growth*

(a) The per capita income and literacy rate of Muslim households is lower as compared to other minorities and Hindus and these were also lower than the all-India average. The people living below poverty line is also high at 43%. Similar is the case about their amenities like 'pucca' house, piped water supply and electric connections. Though the government of India had launched the Prime Minister's 15 Point Programme for the Muslim minorities, which can broadly be classified into 3 categories: security of life and property, reservation in government services and socio-economic development, but because of the conflict between good economy and good politics results are not upto the mark. In order to implement this programme there is a need to set up an independent machinery for planning, execution, monitoring and evaluation of these programmes and necessary budgetary allocations are required to implement them.

(b) Besides this, there is need to set up a Parliamentary Committee separately at the central and states level for supervision of the effectiveness of the programmes and schemes for the minorities. The proposed committees will be required to submit their reports annually before their respective houses during the budget sessions.

(c) In order to improve the availability of capital, National Minorities Development and Finance Corporation at the National level and State Minorities Development and Finance Corporation have been established. However, the ratio of equity-capital contribution both in the central level corporation and state level corporation has to be increased from the present 25% to 49% by the respective governments.

These corporations should also be strengthened on the lines of IDBI, SIDBI and NABARD so as to enable them to borrow from multilateral agencies both soft loans as well as commercial borrowing from domestic market.

3. Empowerment of Muslim Women

(a) *Political Empowerment:* Muslim women are enjoying the status of a minority within a minority. Since the community is educationally and economically backward, it affects seriously the status of Muslim women. The religious orthodoxy, cultural conservatism have added to their misery inspite of the fact that, Islam was the first religion to accept women as a legal entity and accord her rights in matters of marriage, divorce and maintenance. However, the lack of education both secular and religious has relegated their place. It is important that when we are talking of empowerment of women we should concentrate on Muslim women more so as to focus on the real issues of universalization of primary education, adult education, vocational training, better health and hygiene, family planning guidance and economic self-reliance. The government, political parties and the NGOs have added responsibility to bring in more women from the Muslim community to the national mainstream. The much-debated Muslim personal law should be correctly and properly interpreted and applied.

(b) There is a need for proper training of health and family welfare workers in effective counseling techniques to remove misconceptions and anti-family planning attitudes in the Muslim community. At the same time intensive efforts are needed to raise socio-economic and educational status of Muslim people so that they may develop rational attitude towards child bearing and contraception.

(c) Though there is a policy document on the development of women, the focus on Muslim community is lacking. The participation of Muslim women in planning and decision making is very low, so the women organizations who are genuinely working for the upliftment of women should concentrate more on Muslim women's participation in all economic and social activities.

(d) A look at the findings of the recent NHFS data reveals that in the most of the indicators of health i.e. food, nutrition, child care and health awareness the status of Muslim women is relatively better than their counterparts in the majority community. However, as already recommended earlier, they have to be educated more on controlling the size of the family.

(e) A suggestion was also made to provide for reservation of jobs for Muslims in government services, but considering the overall scenario of governmental jobs and trends in global economy where the jobs in government have become too scare and there is a trend to downsize government jobs at all levels, no significant achievement can be made with the suggestion for reservation of jobs to Muslims.

INDEX

❑❑❑